Mothering Multiples

Breastfeeding and
Caring for Twins

Mothering Multiples

Breastfeeding and
Caring for Twins

Karen Kerkhoff Gromada

La Leche League International
Franklin Park, Illinois

July 1985
© 1981, 1985 La Leche League International
All rights reserved
Printed in the United States of America
Illustrations by Jack Cuthbertson
Photo credits:
   Cover and photos on pages 7, 17, 25, 61, 63, 67 © Richard Ebbitt

Library of Congress Catalogue Number 85—080672
ISBN 0-912500-26-3

To my parents — Ed and Peach Kerkhoff

Contents

Preface

Congratulations! Whether you're pregnant or newly delivered, you just found out that it's twins! As the surprise and shock wear off, you are flooded with conflicting emotions. One minute the thought of multiples sounds exciting, and the next minute it seems frightening. Today you may resent getting more than you bargained for. Tomorrow you will be proud of your double dividend. When you are not feeling well, you may get an anxiety attack. Another time, you are in awe that your body can nourish two babies so well.

Questions race through your mind. Will each baby be all right? Will this change the plans for labor and delivery? How will I manage the needs of two babies when one seems a handful? What preparation should I make? What extra equipment is necessary? Can I still nurse even though I'm having two babies?

How do I presume to know how you feel about having twins? I have felt the surprise and numbness myself. I have experienced the ambivalent feelings. And I have asked the questions. I am a mother of twins. I am also a La Leche League Leader of a special group just for mothers who will be or are currently breastfeeding and nurturing multiples. The information in this booklet is a compilation of my experience and those of the other mothers in this group. (I want to give special thanks to my friend and co-Leader, Susan M. Powers, for the long hours she spent typing the manuscript and acting as my sounding board and consultant.)

While re-reading this manuscript before typing, it occurred to me that so much of this seemed to focus on the negative aspects of mothering multiples. I felt frustrated because my overall experience and those of the twin mothers in our League Group were so positive. And then — it suddenly dawned on me. You don't need a book to help you enjoy the fantastic feeling of being the center of two babies' universe — when you approach them and four tiny arms and legs are waving wildly to greet you. Nor do you need advice on how to deal with the intangible pleasure that is yours as you simultaneously feed your twins, while four absorbing eyes never leave your face.

Do I need to describe the awe you feel as you watch two sleeping babies? You don't need to know why you feel so proud when the doctor congratulates you on the babies' good weight gain, and all on mother's milk, too! It's incredible to be given the privilege of eavesdropping on nature's most perfect and interesting environment vs. heredity study, but I don't have to tell you that. It certainly doesn't seem necessary to inform you of all the personal growth you will have as a direct result of dealing with such an intense situation.

The positive aspects of mothering multiples are many-fold, to be experienced with joy. It is for the difficulties that assistance is required. And it is in coping with the difficulties that the most positive personal growth can be achieved.

Good luck and happy mothering, multiplied!

K.K.G.

Note: In this text, he, his, or him will be used in reference to a child. I'm not prejudiced against girl babies; I'm just trying to avoid confusion! Also for the purpose of clarification, the words twin and twins will be used frequently. However, I do not favor the everyday use of these words by the babies' family. "You" generally refers to the twins' mother, but it could be addressing the babies' father quite often. The father's role in nurturing twins is extremely important and it is not my intention to slight these indispensable gentlemen.

Mothering Multiples

Breastfeeding and
Caring for Twins

Chapter One

Discovering It's Twins

H opefully, the diagnosis of twins is made early in the
pregnancy. It will give you time to prepare and deal
with ambivalent feelings. Once you know you are carrying
two babies, you will begin bonding with two babies. Early
diagnosis will also give you time to upgrade your diet, so that
your babies will have the best chance of reaching full-term.

Your nutritional requirements are increased to meet the
needs of two growing babies, and to maintain the health of
one large or two placentas. This means you need to eat
about twice the amount you normally did before your pregnancy.* (Foods high in protein are especially important, but
increases in fats and carbohydrates are also needed.) If you
find it difficult to consume this increased amount because
you feel too full, learn to eat small amounts frequently—

---

*Doubling your intake of food would translate to 130-150 grams pro-
tein and 3100 to 4000 calories per day. When expecting more than two
babies, you should add 30-50 grams protein and at least 500 extra
calories per day for each additional baby. If you are also nursing a toddler, you will need another 20 grams protein and 500 calories per day.

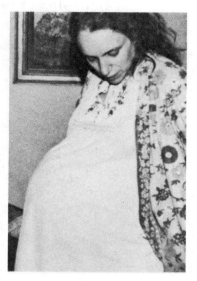

It's no wonder there's little room for meals when you're pregnant with twins!

nibble all day long. Meat, liverwurst, peanut butter, egg salad on whole grain bread or crackers, plus fruit juice or slices of fresh fruit or vegetables each hour is a lightweight snack adding protein, calories, vitamins, and minerals. Milk, eggs, and fruit make a nutritious, high protein milkshake that will not overfill. (Caution is needed with milk and eggs when allergies run in the family.) Soups are another liquid easy on a stomach with little room. Meat, lentil, split pea, and bean soups have good protein content. A weight gain double that of a singleton pregnancy is not unusual when two full-term, normal birthweight babies are expected.

Pregnancy is the ideal time to begin thinking of your twins as two separate, unique persons. Carefully consider the name you give each twin. Some adult twins think "twinnie" names — close sounding, rhyming, or alliterated names — are fun, while others resent it. Some mothers have regretted bestowing "twin" names on their babies, but others have never felt it caused problems. There is no easy way to reach an answer to the question of naming twins.

During the last trimester of your pregnancy, you could begin prenatal nipple care to prepare for breastfeeding. For details, see the section on *Sore Nipples*.

Be sure to discuss questions and concerns with your doctor as well as your husband. The fact that you are expecting twins might greatly change your physician's plans for your labor and delivery. You and your husband have a right to understand the rationale for any changes. Diagnosis of multiples may mean a hospital birth in a delivery room because of positional problems that can occur with more than one baby. Unanesthetized birth is ideal for multiples, especially those born several weeks early. You, your contracting uterus, and gravity can work together to push out each baby, minimizing the need for artificial manipulation, especially of twin number two. But it is your task to clear up all questions related to what you feel is important for a safe and meaningful childbirth experience with your physician. Share with him your concern for the safe delivery of both babies. Cesarean births are slightly more common with multiple pregnancies.

If you do not yet have a physician to care for your babies, now is a good time to shop for one. Many offer a free office visit prior to delivery, but at the very least, talk with the doctor

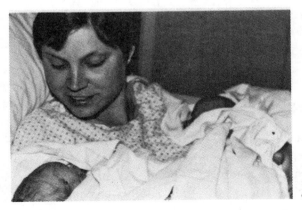

The excitement of having twins also brings conflicting emotions.

Breastfeeding twins gives a mother a feeling of pride and satisfaction.

over the phone. (The office nurse is not an acceptable substitute.) Some questions to consider asking include: What are his ideas about breastfeeding in general, and breastfeeding twins? Does he believe twins can be totally breastfed for their first several months? If one or both babies require special care, could your expressed breast milk be given to them? Would he encourage you to spend time with them in the special care nursery? It is important to carefully choose your babies' doctor, as his support and encouragement of breastfeeding can easily affect your confidence.

Finally, no matter what the circumstances of your babies' birth, it is possible to breastfeed. Mothers have breastfed multiples when they have had a cesarean birth, "surprise twins," premature babies, one or both twins requiring special care, complications related to the delivery, small children at home, little or no household help, work outside the home, or a combination of several of the above. You can feel confident in your body's ability to adapt to your particular situation.

Chapter Two

Deciding to Breastfeed

The advantages of breastfeeding one baby are even more important and intense for multiples. How nice to save twice the money and twice the preparation. And it is twice as nice to curl up at night for feedings in bed, rather than awaken to crying babies who must wait for you to warm their meals. It is rare for totally breastfed babies to get constipated or have diarrhea, so there is no need to keep charts to see which twin is having a BM and when.

Immunity factors in breast milk help protect babies against many diseases. This is important to twins who had to share antibodies passed through the placenta before birth, were born prematurely, or if uterine conditions favored one twin. And a mother of twins with one sick baby may soon have two sick babies.

One advantage is particularly important to you as a mother of multiples. Breastfeeding ensures maximum skin contact with each baby. This is true even if the babies always nurse simultaneously.

No matter how hard you try, it is difficult, if not impossible, to give each twin the time and attention you could give to a single baby. Yet each twin has as many needs as any other baby. Twins do not plan to be born together. Having one another does not replace the need of each for mothering. You cannot expect infants to compromise their needs. This will mean that you and your husband, as the mature members of the family, will have to give more. Breastfeeding is the perfect way to meet the babies' needs for food and their mother's arms.

To maintain an adequate milk supply, you will be forced into close contact with each baby many times a day. Feedings cannot be delegated to others. It is this closeness that will help you relate to and get to know each baby as an individual. They probably will need to eat more often than bottle-fed twins; but with no preparation needed, it just means more cuddling time for them. It's extra time for you to prop your feet up and relax.

One of the most important aspects of breastfeeding is to remember that each baby does not nurse only for food. They may also want to nurse when lonely or frightened. Don't worry if some days are a blur and you feel that, with two babies, you deserve a trophy for breastfeeding marathons!

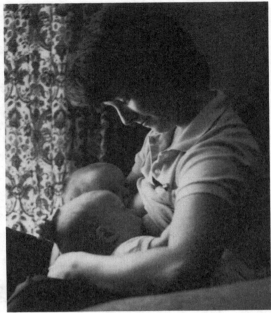

Breastfeeding meets babies' needs in many ways.

These days of frequent feedings are fleeting. What is a brief period of time in *your* life is a very important time in the lives of your infants. It is important work you do, helping your babies adjust to this new world, reinforcing feelings of security and trust. Oh, there are many times when a mother thinks there must be an easier way. But you should consider that most problems are *twin*, not breastfeeding, problems. The rewards of your investment may be postponed (or you may be too busy the first several months to enjoy them), but they do come. And you will get back so much more than you have given!

Breastfeeding twins requires equal amounts of self-confidence and sense of humor. If you are confident that you can produce enough milk, you will — no matter what problems you may have encountered at the start. A sense of humor helps keep babies' needs and the days of breastfeeding marathons in proper perspective!

Breastfeeding ensures maximum skin contact with each baby.

For more information on the physical and emotional advantages of breastfeeding, read La Leche League's book, THE WOMANLY ART OF BREASTFEEDING.

Chapter Three

Adjusting to Twins

Intense is the perfect word to describe life when twins are born into a family. It is a word with positive and negative connotations. One dictionary defines the word *intense* as: 1) occurring or existing in a high degree; very strong, 2) strained to the utmost; earnest, 3) having or showing strong emotion, great seriousness, etc., 4) characterized by much action, emotion, etc. You will probably find nurturing multiples *extremely* intense!

If this is your first mothering experience, give yourself time to learn. Meeting baby needs (times two) while shifting career gears, is a major adjustment. Of course, you will have ambivalent feelings while growing in your new role. Your twins will not realize you have never had *one* baby before, much less two. They don't care that you may be a bit inept — your babies only know that you love them. They know this because you answer when they call, and relieve their hunger in such a pleasant way. They know by your voice when you talk to them, and look into their eyes. All awkwardness is forgiven. Some first-time mothers who have twins feel their situation is *easier,* since they know nothing else!

When you are an experienced mother and remember the time it took to meet the needs of *one* baby, nurturing *two* may seem almost frightening at times. Of course, your other children also have needs; the younger they are, the greater their needs. It is easy to have guilt feelings about the sudden loss of attention the older ones face. At least you feel more relaxed about babies and confident in your mothering. But having felt that wonderful closeness with your previous baby, you may feel totally frustrated when that intimacy seems so elusive with each twin. You realize what a luxury it is to have a moment to take in your baby's face and share that special bond.

Bonding or maternal-infant attachment seems to be very different when you must get to know more than one infant. A woman who has one newborn often feels that intimate closeness within hours, days, or at least within several weeks. When you have two or more healthy newborns, you may find you feel close to or protective of the *unit* of babies first. Once bonded with the unit, you can begin to get acquainted with each unique personality. But don't be surprised if this takes months or even well into the second year — after all, it's difficult to fall in love with two people at the same time!

While this describes the bonding process when two or more healthy babies are born, the attachment process is commonly complicated by factors beyond your control. Multiples undiagnosed until birth, cesarean birth, and prematurity or other conditions requiring special care for one or both babies, with accompanying mother-baby separation, are all situations that can interfere with attachment. Many times one or more of these factors occur in combination. If your twins were a complete surprise, or one baby needed to spend time in the special care nursery while his twin remained with you, it is common to find you feel closer to one baby before the other. Since much of the bond between mother and child forms before birth, it is not surprising that you might think of the first-born twin as "your baby"

*The mother of twins may also have
other children who need her.*

when multiples were unexpected. And isn't it logical to feel close to a baby who was with you constantly and without interruption before you feel close to the baby who must always share you with his twin?

Since these situations are potentially deleterious for the less-favored twin, it is important first to recognize the problem. Now you can do something about it. Don't waste your energy feeling guilty about a situation that began beyond your control. Rather, invest your energy in a positive manner to rectify this problem. Go out of your way to respond immediately to the baby with whom you feel *less* close. Look into his face and talk to him. Make a special effort to increase close contact with him by using a baby carrier, nursing him skin-to-skin in bed, or by taking a bath with him. (Of course, you will still be meeting the needs of the twin you felt closer to.)

Fortunately, as a breastfeeding mother of multiples, you will be in constant intimate contact with each individual, which will help maximize attachment. Perhaps because time is at a premium or bonding can take so much longer, you may find the emotional benefits of breastfeeding postponed for you. This may be disappointing, but remember the babies are enjoying all advantages immediately. Your need to develop a special relationship with each baby is just as important as each baby's need for your special brand of mothering. Be patient — allow breastfeeding and bonding the luxury of *time*.

Lack of time and routine can result in the feeling that you're on a merry-go-round that can't be slowed down, much less stopped. You may find you experience only emotional highs and lows without finding a middle-of-the-road course for quite a while. Sometimes you might feel that your environment, rather than you, is in control. After the birth of a singleton, a new routine begins to emerge after the first month or two. But with two or more babies, everything in your life seems to be in constant change, and it is *much* more difficult to find a routine, or maybe you're too busy to notice one. Unless friends or relatives have had multiples themselves, this can be very difficult for them to understand.

Highs and lows can occur in cycles of days or weeks. When everything is going smoothly, you feel fantastic. You feel proud of the way you are handling the situation and meeting the babies' needs so well. But when two babies take turns crying all day, older children want your attention, the family has been living out of the laundry basket for three days and wash has piled up again, you have used up the last frozen casserole and the cupboards are bare, plus you haven't had more than one and a half hours of sleep at one time for weeks, you are *allowed* to be "in the pits." When you are feeling low, the "guilts" can easily follow. After all, here you are with not one but two beautiful babies. How can anyone so lucky have the right to complain? You are lucky and you know it, but even that does not lessen the intensity of this positive situation or give you more time and sleep.

Of course, much of this depends on your personality, the babies' temperaments, the number and ages of other children, the amount of help you receive, the family situation, etc. But don't be surprised if fluctuations in mood are only high or low, with little in between. Whether you are feeling high or low, remind yourself aloud several times a day, "I am doing the best I can today to cope with this situation."

There is no advice that will eliminate these fluctuations of mood reported by so many new mothers of multiples, but there are ideas that can help you cope:

☐   Enjoy the "highs" when you are feeling so capable of dealing with anything and everything. When experiencing a "low," keep in mind that it will be followed soon by a "high." Just live one day at a time. When even *that* seems too much, live from meal to meal! "I made it through the night to breakfast; I can make it to lunch."

Having two happy, healthy babies makes you feel guilty about complaining at all.

Savor any moments alone with each family member, but realize these time-treasures may be brief. Limited moments will add up, if used wisely.

☐   Take care of yourself. When caring for the needs of so many family members, keep in mind that you have needs, too. If a few minutes of uninterrupted calm come your way, don't think of tonight's menu, the dirty laundry, and the dustballs under the chair. You owe it to yourself to recharge your "giving" batteries by doing something you really enjoy. Cooking, baking, house-cleaning, or something else may be relaxing for you. Go to it! But don't feel guilty if you would rather read, write, nap, sew, bicycle, or jog, etc. The house will fall apart in a different way if you can't satisfy some of your own needs. Just realize these moments of uninterrupted calm will be brief. So don't pick up a novel if you are the sort of person who can't put a good book down, and wait to train for a marathon *next* year or the one after!

☐   While breastfeeding multiples, your nutritional needs will be as great or even greater than during the pregnancy. Supplying two babies with milk is a big business. Most breastfeeding mothers of twins have a tremendous thirst and appetite. If you enjoy food, this is a true advantage of nursing twins. But you wonder how you can meet your nutritional requirements when you have no time for food preparation, much less time for sitting down to enjoy it. The key is easily prepared high protein snacks. Eat while nursing, and always have something to drink available: 1) Cut up fresh fruits and vegetables in quantity when you have some time (or ask someone to do this for you); 2) Cheese cubes and shelled nuts can be taken on the run; 3) Hard boil eggs and eat plain — or make egg salad to spread on whole wheat bread; 4) Fry or scramble an egg in an instant, throw it

on a slice of bread and voila!, high protein. Keep the skillet on the stove and only wash it once or twice a week whether it needs it or not! 5) Each morning make a blender pitcher full of high protein milkshakes and refrigerate for use during the day. These can be egg, fruit, yogurt, wheat germ, milk, etc.; 6) Talk with your physician about taking extra vitamins during lactation. Many mothers find they have more energy when they take more than one prenatal vitamin, in addition to a good diet.

☐   The next time you find tension really building, try one of these socially acceptable physical outlets. Hit tennis balls against a backboard or solid wall. Jump rope indoors or out. Pedal a couple of miles on a stationary or two-wheel bike. Buy some running shoes and hit the road or jog in place at home. (If you decide to try running, alternate walking and running for the first few months. Your body will tell you which to do and when.) Make bread dough and when the recipe states "punch down," really let that dough have it! (This is a most productive release of tension since you will now have something for dinner, too.) All of these activities require a release of physical energy. Surprisingly, you will often discover instead of depleting your energy stores, you have actually *increased* them. None of these activities take much time; all easily fit into any few minutes you can find.

☐   You might find a good cry a wonderful release. Don't feel you must be alone to cry, as it can be most effective in front of others. Anyone present will finally realize you are feeling overwhelmed. You will be treated with renewed respect and tenderness for at *least* an hour!

New mothers often find themselves isolated. Add to this the "Super Mom" myth, the woman who can be all things to all family members at all times, as well as maintain a neat home, and it is no wonder women are afraid to say, "I need some assistance and support." It may be difficult for your husband, friends, and relatives to understand that you will need help when other new mothers are settled in their routines. You might sometimes wonder if you are doing something wrong.

You're doing nothing wrong; you just have twice as many babies as the average new mother! Others may never be able to completely understand the intensity of mothering twins, but it is essential that you learn to ask for their help. You have only yourself to blame if you fail to ask for help when you feel pressured. It is important to take whatever aid is offered by concerned family and friends. *Never deprive someone of the chance to do a good deed.*

Cut all extracurricular activities to the bone while your twins are small. The extra jobs will just add extra pressure. Leaving your babies means each will have *less* of you than he does already, just by being a twin. Your twins will be babies for such a brief time, and all those activities will still be available when you are under less pressure, and your constant presence a little less important.

*Others may have trouble understanding
the intensity of mothering twins.*

It's 4:30 p.m. and you are still in your robe. The flaps of your nursing bra have been down most of the day (including when you opened the door for the delivery man); one of the babies spit up on you at noon; the other waited until 1:30 p.m. to have a bowel movement in your lap; the cup of flour just spilled down the front of your clothing while you were preparing supper; and your husband is due home from work in forty-five minutes. You are not having good feelings at this moment. Unlike the television commercial, you don't have time for a luxurious bubble bath. But the fact is when you look good, you feel good. And when you look like Oscar the Grouch, your mood will suit the name. These ideas will help you maintain "neat and clean" even if you fall short of gorgeous.

Get a "wash and wear" haircut. If possible, get the basic cut about a month before your due date, since twins have been known to arrive early.

Schedule a shower or a quick wash and wipe bath every day. Bathe at about the same time each day, preferably when the babies are napping. If they're awake, put one or both twins in infant seats or automatic swings on the floor in the bathroom or just outside the door. If you sing in the shower, they will enjoy your bathtime as much as you do. A bright mobile over the crib may keep them occupied for the time it takes you to shower. As the babies get older, the portayard (placed just outside the bathroom door) can provide a safe environment for the brief time you are in the tub.

Even if you have lost most of the weight you gained during pregnancy, you might find your body is rearranged! Don't panic — at least not yet. It took months to gain that weight during pregnancy. If your diet was balanced during pregnancy and continues to be balanced now, almost everything will shift back into shape eventually. In the meantime, try to stretch the budget to purchase some new clothing that will fit while you *s l o w l y* shrink. You'll think thinner in clothing that fits.

If your twins were born at full term and their combined weight was well over ten or eleven pounds, you may find yourself suffering from what those in the mothering multiples trade refer to as "twin skin." You know you have it if your stretch marks have stretch marks, your abdomen looks like accordion pleats, and you can pull out your abdominal skin, fold it up, and tuck it into your pants or skirt! The skin on your abdomen has lost some of its elasticity. Learn to camouflage it with clothing. Overblouses and sweaters cover a multitude of sins. When you tuck a shirt in your slacks or skirt, lift your hands over your head to loosen the material around your waist. Dark clothing makes you look trimmer than pale colors. A wide belt will give you a much leaner look than a thin one.

Whether you have few or many pounds to lose, exercise will help you look your best. Sit-ups and leg lifts to tone abdominal muscles take just a few minutes several times a week. (Check with your doctor on when to safely begin these.) Jogging, jumping rope, or pushing a fifteen-pound stroller carrying two babies will help you get back in shape.

*Wearing two piece outfits
helps you to nurse discreetly*

You'll probably find two-piece outfits most convenient for discreet breastfeeding. Keep this in mind when buying clothing. Lift the top enough for the baby to latch on to the breast; his body will cover you. But you could use a diaper, receiving blanket, or shawl to ensure that you are not exposed while you gain confidence. It is often difficult to nurse twins simultaneously in public, but some mothers even manage this. The position that most lends itself to this is to place one baby in the traditional nursing position, while the second baby rests his head on the abdomen of the first with his body in the football-hold position. Again a diaper, blanket, or shawl will help cover the three of you.

If you were on the small side prior to pregnancy, you might enjoy your expanded bustline during lactation. But if you were amply endowed, your current size may seem like too much of a good thing. Often the main problem for large-breasted women is finding a nursing bra that provides proper support. Sometimes the major department store chains, which also have a large catalog business, carry larger size nursing bras in their catalogs than you can find in the stores. Other mothers buy a good supportive standard-type brassiere and then cut a circle large enough for the areola and nipple to protrude. Be sure the circle is large enough for skin-to-skin contact during feedings, and stitch around to reinforce the material. When buying nursing bras with flaps, be sure to find ones that release the flap with a flick of a finger. It can be hard enough to juggle two babies without trying to undo tricky hooks.

When milk leakage is a problem in the early months, there are several alternatives to the expensive nursing pads sold. Your husband's white handkerchiefs will work; though if you leak very much, washing all those hankies is one more thing you can do without when caring for twins. Disposable diapers (minus their plastic lining) or sanitary napkins can be cut and used, although you may find that some contain perfumes or deodorants which can be irritating to nipples. White paper towels can be folded in half lengthwise, and then into thirds for use as nursing pads. Try different brands, as some are softer than others. All of these options are fairly low in price and can be thrown away without one being too concerned about cost. You will probably want to buy at least one box of nursing pads to wear when you are "out" with the babies.

Remember all the money you are saving by breastfeeding your twins when you have second thoughts about spending money on yourself buying new clothing, or supportive nursing bras, or getting a new wash and wear haircut. You are worth it. And the whole family benefits when you feel good about yourself.

You may find that vaginal bleeding after delivery of multiples is heavier and/or lasts longer. This might concern you, particularly if this is not your first childbirth experience. However, one very large or two normal placentas cover a much larger area of the uterus. As the placenta site heals, it is normal to expect a bit more bleeding. A uterus that wants to relax due to over-distention can also be a problem. Of course, breastfeeding is the best thing possible since the release of the hormone, oxytocin (which causes "let

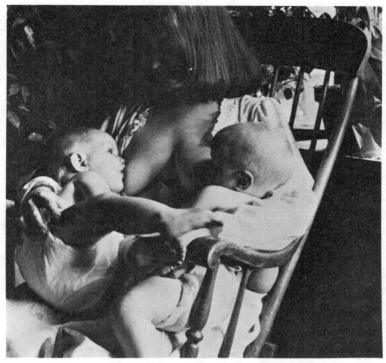

The mother of twins will make good use of a comfortable rocking chair for soothing and nursing babies.

down"), also causes uterine contractions that constrict blood vessels at the placental site and enhance involution or shrinking of the uterus.

The length of time that lactation suppresses ovulation varies as much among mothers of multiples as mothers of singletons. Having twice as many babies does not necessarily mean twice as long until your menstrual cycle resumes. However, you might experience a later return of ovulation while breastfeeding twins than a singleton. Total breastfeeding during the first several months, delayed solids, nighttime nursings, etc., are likely to influence a delay in a return of the menses.

Chapter Four

Breastfeeding Twins

Getting Started

I f both babies are in good condition at birth, breastfeed as soon as possible. Immediately after birth is the best time to start. If both babies require special care, begin expressing your milk ten to twelve times per day within twenty-four hours of the twins' birth. It is better to express your milk ten to twelve times per day for ten to twenty minutes, than to empty your breasts only four or six times a day but for thirty to forty minutes.

When one baby is in the special care nursery, express your milk or pump one breast while nursing a baby on the other breast. This allows you to get the maximum benefit from your let-down. Whether one or both babies require special care, your expressed milk should be given to them. Keep this breast milk in sterile glass or plastic containers marked with your name, date, and time of expression. Refrigeration is all that is required for breast milk that will be given to a baby within forty-eight hours. Otherwise, store your milk in a freezer until needed. Store in a zero degree or deep-freeze if this period will be over two weeks. Call an LLL Leader for more help and support with milk expression and storage.

Room-in with your twins if both are in good condition. Unless one or both are in the special care nursery, ask that *both* babies be brought to you for *all* feedings. You need to see them together to know this is real and to begin getting to know each as an individual. Also, it is unrealistic to think you can build a milk supply for two babies if only one is brought per feeding. (You can make up for lost time when you get home, but it is easier if you get off to a good start.)

Ideas for getting off to an optimum breastfeeding start can be implemented even after a cesarean birth. When both babies are in good condition and a spinal anesthetic was used for delivery, nursing personnel can help you roll over to one side. Pillows or a rolled blanket at your back will help keep you in position. If on your right side, nurse one baby at your right breast. When he is finished, raise the second baby to your left breast by propping him on a pillow. You can even sit up to nurse if you've had an epidural. Breastfeeding immediately after a cesarean delivery is ideal since the anesthetic will keep you comfortable. You might need help from the nurses for the first day or two with breastfeeding or expressing milk for babies in a special care nursery, but it is important to begin stimulating your milk supply. Rooming-in, whether partial or round-the-clock, should be feasible after the first few days.

Coordinating Feedings

This entire "learning period" does take a good four to seven months — so do keep this in mind. These are just suggestions and the most common means of coordinating breastfeeding. But almost anything will work. You will be amazed at the adaptability of the female body!

Learning to nurse the twins simultaneously takes practice.

Use both breasts for each baby, each feeding. Feed Baby A on the right breast for about ten minutes and let him finish on the left breast. Baby B starts on the left breast, nurses about ten minutes and finishes at the right breast. After the milk supply is well established, you may find that using both breasts causes overfeeding. Switch to just one breast per feeding if this happens. (Incidentally, when Baby B starts to breastfeed, you do experience a second let-down.)

Use the right breast for Baby A and the left breast for Baby B, and rotate the next day so that Baby A nurses at the left breast and Baby B at the right. This is a popular way of coordinating feedings. Both babies stimulate the milk supply of both breasts — without complicating matters trying to remember who nursed where and when.

Nurse the hungriest baby on the fullest breast. Your let-down reflex will conform to babies' needs, and you can have one let-down after another.

Some mothers assign a baby the same breast for all feedings after the milk supply is well established, or if one baby prefers a certain breast for a period of time. Though few women report a major discrepancy in breast size due to differing milk supplies, assigning each baby a specific breast **may** present problems. If for any reason one baby could not nurse for even a short time, the other might balk at the request to feed at both breasts. Of even more importance is the fact that when a baby is held in the same position for all feedings, only one of his eyes receives adequate exercise. Therefore, it is necessary to alternate positions for feedings.

Simultaneous Breastfeeding

The decision to nurse both babies together is as much theirs to make as yours. Some babies latch on quite well; others need much help for several months. Some babies will refuse to cooperate with simultaneous feedings, while another baby will refuse to nurse until he hears his twin sucking at the other side! Experiment with different nursing posi-

Twin on the right is in the traditional nursing position; twin on the left is in the "football hold" with legs under mother's arm.

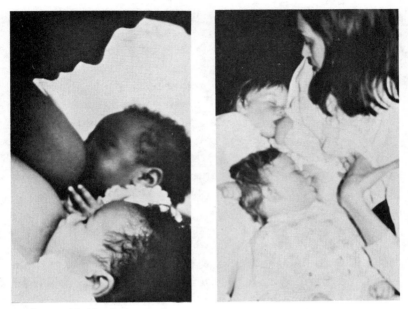

*Mothers and babies find a way to
nurse simultaneously.*

tions and pillows until you find one that works best for you
and your babies.

Few mothers nurse their babies simultaneously every
feeding, nor do most nurse them separately every time. Like
other aspects of breastfeeding, the beauty of simultaneously
nursing is in its adaptability to meet your babies' changing
needs. When the babies have too much difficulty breastfeeding simultaneously, but both are hungry at the same time —
at least touch Baby B, while feeding Baby A. (See section on
Fussy Baby.) If simultaneous nursing is not practical during
one period of infancy, you might want to try again at a later
date.

Most mothers find that identical twins tend to fall into
the same routine without help from Mom. Simultaneous
feedings are very helpful in this situation, as it is heart-
breaking to be feeding Baby A while listening to Baby B cry

because he is also hungry. You can't enjoy nursing "A" because you feel so frustrated and unhappy about "B." Baby A is often rushed through the feeding and then you feel guilty about *that!*

With fraternal twins who might naturally be in very different routines, you may find it saves time to wake one twin and feed him along with the other. Or you could nurse one baby alone, then awaken and nurse the other. There are pros and cons regarding the possibility of disturbing a baby's natural rhythm. On one hand, feeding babies together or one after the other may give you some time for yourself and other family members. But it means you must always deal with two babies when they are awake — which can be overwhelming. On the other hand, just holding one baby and looking into his face is a luxury to be enjoyed. But it often means you are constantly caring for a baby, as one will wake just as the first falls asleep. Also, by not allowing them to wake up in their *own* time, you might miss the baby ready for a longer nap or nighttime sleep. Some free-thinking babies will have nothing to do with manipulation of their natural routines, and for you to continue trying to manipulate will lead to extra work and frustration.

If you decide to breastfeed your twins simultaneously because they are hungry at the same time or because it makes the situation easier for you to handle, do not worry that you are not spending time with each individual baby. (It may be *months* before the babies realize or care that someone else is on the other breast.) There is no reason why you can't look into one baby's face and talk with him for a few minutes, and then do the same with the other. It will be easier to get to know each baby since feedings can be leisurely and relaxed. Remember though, that it's harder to remove the nipple from baby's mouth when simultaneously nursing.

COMMON SIMULTANEOUS FEEDING POSITIONS:

☐   Baby A is in the traditional nursing position with Baby B's head on A's abdomen. Baby B's body is held in the football-hold position. This is the most inconspicuous position, and the one most easily mastered, if one (or both) has difficulty latching on to the breast. *(The football hold means baby faces you while his body is tucked under your arm or at a 90° angle to your body. Pillows to support baby's body are necessary to avoid arm strain.)* It might be easier to place the second baby in the football-hold on your dominant side. For example if you are right handed, place Baby A on the left breast in the traditional nursing position. With Baby B propped on A's abdomen and a pillow, your dominant right hand will be free to help him latch on to the right breast. (Of course, you would reverse this, if left handed.) Also, a mother should switch babies around for eye exercise and not always put the second baby in the football-hold on her dominant side.

☐   Both babies nurse in traditional position with bodies criss-crossed or supported by your thighs. A footstool to prop your feet sometimes helps, or breastfeed while tailor-sitting. A reclining chair accommodates three very nicely, you can sleep in it, and the footstool is built right in. (A beanbag chair is also great, because it can support all of you in comfort.)

☐   Hold *both* babies in the football-hold position. This position is beneficial if you've had a cesarean birth and want to avoid pressure on the incision area. If you use pillows on your lap and at your sides to support babies' heads as well as their bodies, you will have two free hands to read a story to older siblings, eat a snack, or look something up in this book.

☐   Mom lies on stomach propped on elbows — nurse both and possibly read a bit. (This is the least-used simultaneous position.)

This mother uses pillows to position both babies in the traditional nursing position with their bodies criss-crossed.

☐   If babies have difficulty latching on, you can breast-feed simultaneously when someone else is available to help. Have someone hold Baby A's head in place after latching on, while you help Baby B get started.

Older baby or toddler twins will often demand to nurse together, simultaneously, in their drive for equality. This sometimes results in a "play or punch" session with you feeling in the middle of a mini-tornado! Put a rattle or other small toy at each end of a string or ribbon around your neck. This diversion might help all involved to get back down to business. If this doesn't work, you may have to enforce a one-at-a-time rule for a few weeks or months. Sometimes it is enough to say, "No," put them down for a few minutes, and then resume the nursing. It's important to be consistent.

Night Feedings

In general, the nearer you can keep the babies to your bed, the easier it is on all of you. You'll probably need only one crib (or none) for the first three to six months. Many twins sleep better if they are touching each other. It will save you steps if the crib is in your bedroom or they are in bed with you. If that's not possible, put an extra mattress in the babies' room for your night feedings. As soon as possible, double or triple-diaper the twins to avoid nighttime changes. The following are alternative ways of night nursing:

☐   Feed Baby A and then fall asleep until Baby B awakens. Settle Baby A down and fall asleep while nursing Baby B.

☐   Nurse Baby A and settle him then awaken Baby B and nurse him.

☐   Remove one side-rail from the crib. Adjust the crib mattress to the level of your mattress and fasten securely against your bed. One baby can sleep between you and your husband, while the other sleeps in the crib. Roll from side to side to meet breastfeeding needs during the night.

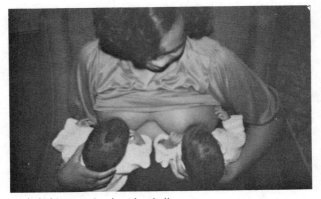

Both babies are in the "football hold" position with mother supporting one head with each hand.

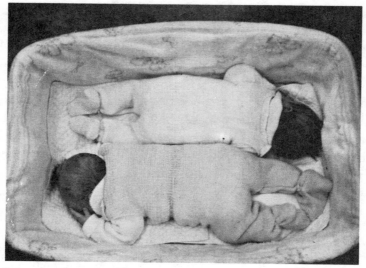

*Twins sleep best when they can
cuddle up together.*

With newborns, simultaneous nursing is difficult while
lying down. You will probably have to sit up against a
bedrest pillow or in a chair until your babies are several
months old, if they need to be fed at the same time. Later
on, you can try to place pillows parallel to your body, with
one baby lying on each pillow, and nurse from this position.
(You would be on your back, of course.) The benefits of a
king-size bed cannot be underestimated when it comes to the
ease of having the twins sleep between the parents!

Chapter Five

Establishing a Good Supply of Milk

The Need for Supplements

A supplement may be defined as anything other than your milk which you feed your babies. This would include formula, water, or solids before the middle of the first year. There are few mothers of twins who cannot produce enough breast milk for both babies, once they have gotten off to a good start. Early, frequent breastfeeding (or milk expression if babies need special care), plus your understanding that the more babies nurse — the more milk you will make — are usually enough to produce an abundance of breast milk.

Supplements may be necessary initially if breastfeeding twins got off to a slow start — a problem all too common with multiples. (Nursing only one baby per feeding, no night nursings, cesarean delivery, or separation from one or both babies because they need to be in the special care nursery are all examples of what could contribute to a slow start.) When you bring the twins home after a poor beginning, the best possible treatment is to take the twins to bed with you for several days of round-the-clock nursing on demand. You will probably find you are bursting with milk and babies' demands have decreased a little by the end of a week.

If your poor start means rebuilding a milk supply virtually from scratch, or your twins have a bad case of mother vs. rubber-nipple confusion causing them to resist the breast, supplements may be needed while solving these problems. Rarely will it be necessary to supplement on an ongoing basis.

When low milk supply is the problem, but babies have no difficulty latching on, you might try these suggestions:

☐   Nurse each twin ten to twelve times per day, simultaneously or individually.

☐   Each baby should be producing six to eight soaking wet diapers per day. Keeping track of the diaper count will help you determine the least amount of supplement you can give.

☐   It should not be necessary to supplement after each feeding. Often one or two supplementary feedings a day is enough. Giving too many supplements interferes with the supply and demand of making milk, undermines your confidence, and wastes your precious time!

☐   Gradually eliminate supplements by deleting one ounce in each bottle about every five days. Expect the babies to nurse an extra time or two the first couple of days. You can subtract another ounce per bottle when they fall back into their regular routines and the diaper count picks up again.

Difficulty latching on to the breast or nipple confusion can be very frustrating problems to overcome, especially when you are caring for two newborns. A weak sucking reflex is more common when twins have been born prematurely or had other complications at birth. This can be compounded by separation from you in a special care nursery. The unnecessary introduction of rubber nipples on unnecessary supplements can also cause this problem with babies born full term!

☐   A baby must use completely different jaw and tongue movements for breastfeeding and bottle-feeding. Going back and forth from breast to bottle can be very confusing. It is better to spoon-feed supplements to a baby with nipple confusion. This lets baby know that if he wants the pleasure of sucking, it must be at the breast. If it seems there are not enough hours in the day to allow for spoon feeding each time, at least use an orthodontic (Nuk) nipple on the bottle.

☐   Always attempt to nurse before offering a supplement. Relax, be patient, and don't worry if baby has difficulty latching on at first. The magic moment *will* come soon when he figures out how to get that good milk from your warm breast.

☐   Put the baby to your breast whenever you notice him making sucking movements — even in his sleep.

☐   Continue to express your milk manually or with a breast pump so that you are emptying your breasts at least ten to twelve times a day. Always give the babies your milk before *anything* else.

☐   If only one has difficulty with your nipple, try him simultaneously with his twin. The baby with a good sucking pattern will stimulate a stronger let-down which sometimes forces the "weaker" twin to move his mouth correctly to swallow all that milk. At best, things may improve as soon as he figures out what he must do. At worst, he will cough, sputter, and let go of the breast.

☐   When one baby nurses well, pump on the other side while he sucks. The stronger let-down (initiated by this twin) will usually result in more breast milk to supplement the other while he is learning to nurse.

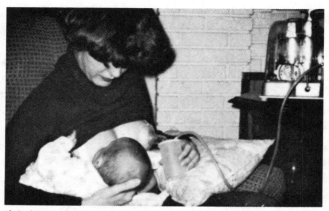

If it is necessary to pump your milk, you can nurse one baby and pump milk from the other breast.

Slow Weight Gain

Many a new mother worries about the amount of weight her baby gains, especially if this is her first breastfeeding experience. It takes a while to gain confidence in her own body. When you have twins, it may take even longer to acquire the confidence to trust your body to produce enough milk. According to THE WOMANLY ART OF BREAST-FEEDING, an average of one pound per month, or four to seven ounces per week per baby, is a good weight gain. A little less in a given week or month should not be reason for concern. As long as each baby steadily gains weight, albeit slowly, it is probably perfectly normal. (Measure baby's weight gains from lowest weight *after* birth—not birth weight.) It can be fascinating watching fraternal twins who get the same milk develop at totally different rates. Sometimes one can gain several pounds a month while the other barely a pound, but both are perfectly healthy. However, there are times when one or both babies are not gaining enough weight. Whether the problem lies with one or both twins, here is a checklist that might help you increase your milk supply, and subsequently, your babies' weights:

● Sometimes a poor start at breastfeeding and lack of breastfeeding know-how result in improper weight gain. It is important to understand that your milk supply works on a supply and demand basis. In other words, the more the babies nurse, the more milk your body will make. It is normal for each baby to nurse at least eight to twelve times a day. Each should be soaking six to eight diapers every day. When babies *aren't* gaining, be sure to nurse them at least every two hours during the day, and about every three hours at night. Set the alarm if necessary. You have to step up the number of feedings, even if you must wake the babies to do it.

● Poor sucking on a baby's part could mean he cannot empty the breast sufficiently. Each twin should have a good mouthful of the areola, the dark area that surrounds the actual nipple. It should be difficult to break the suction to remove the baby's mouth. When he has a good grasp of the nipple, he will not easily let go. Sore nipples for you may accompany improper nursing patterns.

● Your diet must consist of nutritious food to maintain an adequate milk supply for two babies. Write down all that you've eaten in the last two days. Hopefully, you are looking at a diet comprised of fresh fruits and vegetables, whole grains, dairy products, meat, fish, and eggs. Your fluid intake should be high. A mother totally breastfeeding twins can easily drink two to three quarts of fluid a day. (If you are getting enough liquid, your urine will be very pale yellow or almost clear.) Be sure to go easy on caffeinated beverages like coffee, tea, most soft drinks, and diet soft drinks. These have a diuretic effect which deplete the body fluids.

You may find taking brewer's yeast helpful; follow the directions on the label.

● You might be trying to do too much, too soon, and succumbing to the "Super Mom" myth. You shouldn't be worrying about all that needs to be done around the house, or you might find you are rushing babies through feedings. Your twins will be babies such a short time, and you can clean the dustballs or bake cookies for the charity bazaar later.

● Babies need lots of skin contact between feedings, as well as while nursing. It is not enough to see that babies are fed and have dry diapers. Each baby thrives on your closeness, as well as the milk you provide. You cannot hold and cuddle your babies *too* much. After all, how much is too much love?

● A baby who is not gaining weight should never use a pacifier. He needs to satisfy his sucking needs at the breast to increase your milk supply. It is not a good idea to offer water as a supplement. Giving water interferes with a diaper count. *(Water is unnecessary, as breast milk is 80-90% water.)*

After reading through the suggestions of what you can do to increase your milk supply, *believe* that you can do it! It takes motivation for any mother to increase her milk supply with one baby, much less two. Occasionally, a mother of twins will find she cannot cope with the extra work required. Or rarely a baby will not gain even though you have done everything to correct the problem. If either is the case, you might find it necessary to start some solid food once or twice a day.

Even if you and your babies' physician decide a supplement is necessary for a while in your situation, it does not mean that weaning is inevitable.

This mother holds both babies in the "football hold" position with each baby supported by pillows.

☐   Supplementing only once or twice a day is often just as effective in stimulating babies' growth spurts as several supplements a day. Frequent supplementary feedings will cause your milk supply to decrease even more because it interferes with the supply and demand basis of making milk. Because it is also very time-consuming, you may soon feel one or the other must be given up. Since you know your milk supply is still low for two babies, breastfeeding is often dropped.

☐   A little mashed banana or rice cereal, diluted with breast milk, may be a better supplement than formula. Nipple confusion can also be avoided when a small amount of solid food is given.

☐   Once babies are gaining properly, supplements can often be decreased by omitting an ounce of formula or a small amount of solids per supplementary feeding every few days. (Meanwhile, you have been following the guidelines for increasing your milk supply.) Don't be surprised if babies want to nurse more for a couple of days following every time you decrease the supplement. Babies should continue having six to eight soaking wet diapers every day.

☐   Be sure to discuss these ideas for increasing your milk supply and supplementing your babies' diets with their doctor. When he realizes how important breastfeeding is to you and your babies, and understands the rationale for building your milk supply, he is less likely to recommend too-frequent supplements. He may want to see the twins more often until the weight-gain problem is resolved. Should either of your twins have a problem of slow or no weight gain, call an LLL Leader for help and additional information.

Points to Consider

There may be a day when you feel willing to try anything to calm two crying babies. A supplement may look very tempting when babies are crying, you think your milk supply is low, and your confidence is even lower. You may think a supplement will help you get extra rest after the delivery, especially if it was a cesarean birth. Just one good night's sleep can sound very appealing.

You may experience pressure from husband, friends, relatives, or even doctors to supplement because they think it is impossible to supply two babies totally with breast milk. They may worry that breastfeeding is too hard on you.

Confidence is the key in avoiding supplements for these reasons. Often supplements will further complicate your hectic lifestyle. When you consider that all alternatives to breastfeeding require preparation, warming, and clean-up, then you can understand that nursing is easier and gives you more time to relax with your babies. This is especially true when you realize babies' needs for mother's arms during feedings. Let your husband, family, and friends know how much it means to you to breastfeed. What you may need is more support from them — not necessarily a supplement for a baby.

If you are occasionally supplementing (or the temptation is there), consider these important points:

Many of the physical advantages of breastfeeding are compromised by introducing a foreign substance, even occasionally. Respiratory, gastrointestinal, and other bacterial or viral infections are more common when babies are given formula supplements. Frequent supplementation of breast milk can contribute to anemia. Each time something other than mother's milk is given to a young baby, he is being exposed to a potential allergen. Breastfeeding produces a very delicate balance in a baby's body which can easily be disrupted.

The best indication that you are producing enough milk are babies' wet diapers. You should be changing six to eight soaking wet diapers per baby each day. (Don't mislead the diaper count by giving unnecessary supplemental water.)

Keep in mind the proven fact that solids given at bedtime do *not* affect nighttime waking patterns of babies.

It is normal for each baby to nurse eight to twelve times per day. But different babies have different breastfeeding needs. It may seem confusing if each of your babies has a different nursing pattern. Don't worry about the number of hours between nursings.

Very often babies are breastfed, and satisfied, in the time it would have taken to warm a supplement.

Frequent breastfeeding increases your milk supply. It does not mean your milk supply is deficient. Babies often nurse for reasons other than hunger.

Some mothers express their milk (or collect leakage) in a

> cup at the same time as nursing one twin alone. They use this when they feel their milk supply is low, or they need a few hours of uninterrupted sleep.

> Your husband can help with night feedings by bringing the babies to you for feeding, changing diapers, cuddling one twin while you're feeding the other, etc.

As with other aspects of parenting, the decision to supplement is yours to make. It is important to look at all possible aspects of this situation to make the best decision for your babies.

If for any reason you discontinue breastfeeding altogether, it does not change your twins' need for your presence. It is very important that you hold and cuddle each of them for feedings. Babies learn to trust and feel secure with the mother who replaces hunger pains with a pleasurable fullness. Using baby carriers, and spending time in a rocking chair, are other means of obtaining close contact with your infants.

It is *not* a good idea to totally breastfeed one twin and totally bottle feed the other. This would mean one receives perfect nutrition and immunity factors, while the other is exposed to a potential allergen and obtains no disease protection. Most importantly, this could be detrimental to the maternal-infant attachment process. Breastfeeding is a gift of self to a baby, as well as providing close contact and nutrition. It would be better to breastfeed *both* as much as possible and supplement *both*, if necessary. Sometimes only *one* baby needs a supplement (are there enough wet diapers?), but is also breastfed until the milk supply builds. But, don't make this an all or nothing situation. Suspect "nursing strike" if early weaning of one twin seems to be occurring. (See *Nursing Strike.*)

Meeting Sucking Needs

You may find it difficult at times to completely meet the sucking needs of multiples by breastfeeding. There simply may not be enough time to allow unlimited sucking at the breast. Or you may find you produce so much milk that the babies get extremely full and/or spit up, if sucking time is not limited.

☐ If over-production is the problem, offer only one breast per baby at a feeding. Limit sucking time to ten or fifteen minutes *only* if absolutely necessary.

☐ When limiting time at the breast for any reason, an orthodontic type pacifier to meet babies' sucking needs can be helpful. This kind of pacifier stimulates baby to use the same muscles in almost the same way as at the breast.

☐ Thumb or finger sucking is a common way that one or both twins find to meet their oral needs.

☐ As much as possible, hold and cuddle the babies when offering a pacifier. *A "thing" cannot take the place of your arms.*

It's not unusual for twins to suck their thumbs to meet sucking needs.

Dad can help feed the twins when
they start solids.

Growth Spurts and Starting Solids

Growth spurts commonly occur at approximately six weeks, three months, and six months, with a frequency day thrown in any time. Your babies are saying they need more breast milk to meet their nutritional needs by nursing more often than usual during these periods. These growth spurts, or frequency days, can occur for both twins at the same time or at different times. This can be quite confusing!

If you are wondering whether your twins are getting enough milk, stop and examine the situation. Just the realization that you are in the midst of a growth spurt or a frequency day can help you weather this challenge. Understand that these periods of frequent feedings rarely last more than a week; this is several days longer than the usual growth spurt for a singleton. This is generally not the time to start solid foods or supplement, but it is important to allow the babies (or baby) extra nursing so your milk supply can increase to meet their needs. *Let each baby be your guide.* (Fortunately, most growth spurts are followed by a period of relative calm.)

Mothers of twins sometimes start giving solid food *earlier* than mothers of singletons. It's often begun earlier than necessary because of pressure from others, or the feeling that anything is worth a try during a particularly overwhelming period. In general, twins have no more need than singletons for solid food until sometime during the middle of the first year. This has nothing to do with their combined weight. Each twin may show a readiness for solids at a different time in the first year, especially if fraternal twins. Don't bother with solids for the one who is not ready.

If both babies are ready for solids at the same time, be sure to start very slowly. Too much, too soon can be a big shock to your babies' digestive systems. (Too many solids, too soon, can also be a big shock to your milk supply, which can lead to a plugged duct or even a breast infection.) When one or both begin taking solids, always nurse first, then offer solids. Once the babies get used to eating from a spoon, you can put them in infant seats or high chairs, using one bowl and one spoon and alternate bites and babies. Switch to finger foods as soon as possible and get out of their way!

With full-term twins there is probably no more reason to give supplemental vitamins or iron than with any single full-term baby. However, the babies' doctor may want to be more careful if the twins were premature or environmental conditions in utero favored *one* twin. Sometimes one twin receives a disproportionate share of nutrients before birth. A simple blood test done in the physician's office can determine a need of one or both babies for additional iron.

Chapter Six

Avoiding Breastfeeding Problems

Sore Nipples

Even though you are nursing more than one baby, your chances of getting sore nipples are not any greater than a mother having a single baby. However, it may take longer for sore nipples to heal should they become a problem. It is not known whether this is due to so much stimulation, or lack of time to work through solutions. Remember that rest is essential in getting over sore nipples. Here are some ideas that should take no extra time:

If you are still pregnant, prenatal nipple care described in THE WOMANLY ART OF BREASTFEEDING may be helpful. Discontinue the use of soap to wash your breasts; plain water is fine. *The best preventive measure is a good breastfeeding start when your babies are born.* Nursing immediately after birth and frequently thereafter can greatly diminish this problem. If your babies need special care — cannot nurse right after birth — early frequent expression of milk will help lessen the chance of sore nipples.

After feedings, leave the flaps of your nursing bra down, so that the nipples are exposed to the air. Alternate feeding positions to rotate strong suction placement. Though it may seem contradictory, frequent nursings are beneficial. You may think holding the babies off will give your nipples more time to heal, but this can actually cause more soreness because ravenously hungry babies have difficulty latching on to overfull breasts. If nipples become too sore or there is any cracking it may be necessary to employ the frequent feedings, while limiting sucking time to ten or fifteen minutes, until the nipples heal. When sore, red nipples persist you might suspect a fungus infection.

Plugged Ducts and Breast Infections

Plugged ducts and breast infections seem to be no more a problem for the mother of twins than for the mother of a single infant. However, factors that can contribute to plugged milk ducts and breast infections are more likely, and may have a greater effect on you with a double milk supply. *Fatigue, tension, trying to get too much done, poor nutrition, and missing feedings can make you more prone to any of these problems.*

If you get a plugged duct or breast infection, apply warm, wet compresses to the site, and nurse frequently on the affected side to ensure that the breast remains as empty as possible. You may find taking extra vitamin C helpful.

Biting

Biting is much more common with breastfeeding twins than singletons during the second half of the first year. However, biting can be overcome. Babies do not have to bite down in order to remove milk. It should not be necessary to discontinue breastfeeding for this problem. Consistent handling is the key. Firmly and emotionally say, "No," or "Ouch!" if a baby bites down. (This does not require much thought!) Immediately break the suction to remove the baby from the breast, and put him down. If he still seems interested in nursing, a few minutes later offer the breast again. Repeat the procedure as necessary. It rarely takes much time to prove your point. *It might be necessary to breastfeed each twin individually while solving this uncomfortable predicament! Your firm "No!" will also startle the innocent twin. It can be difficult to put one down, and then let him nurse a few minutes later if you have been feeding simultaneously.* If biting occurs at the end of a feeding, your baby is telling you he's finished. So, when you see him slowing down, end the feeding before he's bored and bites. Remember, older babies are very efficient and can empty a breast in just a few minutes.

Nursing Strikes

When a baby refuses to nurse, it is called a "nursing strike." This seems fairly common with twins. It generally involves just one twin—often the more patient of the two. If a strike occurs, it is most common in the last half of the first year. Try to determine the cause when a baby goes on strike. A baby who has been sick and had difficulty nursing, or a teething baby, will sometimes go on strike. Your baby may protest if your lowered milk supply indicates you may have

been doing too much. The baby who is willing to wait for his feeding, or is more agreeable when he is rushed through a nursing so you can put his twin to breast, may finally put his foot down by "striking." Combine breastfeeding with extra skin contact to help this baby get back to the breast. Feed him in a quiet room away from distraction whenever possible. Breastfeed nude from the waist up, with the baby wearing only a diaper, or take this baby into a tub of warm water with you. (The bath is relaxing, the breast is available.) You could also put the baby to breast while he is still asleep, before he realizes what he is doing. If this twin prefers a certain breast, assign that breast to him, and the other breast to his twin. (Alternate nursing positions if each baby always nurses at the same breast.) Try to stay relaxed and calm, and allow the non-striking twin to help out by nursing frequently to keep you from getting overfull.

Chapter Seven

Comforting a Fussy Baby

J ust like singletons, one or both twins can have fussy times that last hours. Twins can have colic. If fussiness occurs at a different time during the day for each baby, you may feel like the day is one long fussy time. And you're more than half right! On the other hand, when fussy periods occur at the same time, it is *extremely* frustrating to cope with two crying babies.

Any mother who has felt the helplessness and frustration of dealing with *one* fussy or uncomfortable baby, can only imagine contending with *two*. Even if only one baby is fussy, you must cope with that twin, plus meet the needs of the other. It is more than doubly frustrating.

This is often the point when you feel ready to throw in the towel, put the babies in cribs or automatic swings, walk away, and let the babies cry it out. It may be very difficult for you to take the broader viewpoint. But letting them cry it out will only teach the babies that you are not there when they need you most. *No matter how frustrated and overwhelmed you feel, the twins are feeling even more so!* Imagine how terrible it would be to feel uncomfortable and not know why or even how to communicate the nature of the discomfort. Babies don't *choose* to be fussy.

Hopefully these ideas will help you survive the fussy times:

● Hold and cuddle your babies. Try using your breast as a pacifier, but don't feel rejected if this is not what the uncomfortable baby wants. Cuddling or nursing may not relieve babies' discomfort, but at least they know you are there and you care.

● Many babies have fussy periods. This is rarely a breastfeeding problem, but check your diet for things that could affect the babies through your milk. Try eliminating any suspicious food and see what happens. Some babies are sensitive to cow's milk products or eggs that you eat, especially if there is a history of allergies on either side of the family. Formula supplements could cause fussiness. Other babies have negative reactions to supplemental vitamins, iron, and fluorides. You might want to watch your intake of caffeinated beverages. This would include most soft drinks and diet soft drinks, as well as coffee and tea. Smoke from cigarettes can irritate your baby and the nicotine and other chemicals are excreted in your milk. It can even decrease the milk supply if you are a heavy smoker. Oral contraceptive pills and medicated IUDs can affect the quality and quantity of your breast milk. Deodorants, insect-, furniture-, hairsprays, etc., and baby powder are inhalants which can get into your bloodstream and milk and disturb babies. (A *baby* can be bothered if you use sprays in his presence, too.) Experiment to see if any of these things are causing babies' distress. It's important to remember that twins are two individuals. Just because something does not irritate one, it could still irritate or cause fussiness in the other.

● Place the fussy twin in a baby carrier that is constructed to be worn on the front or back. He can be carried in front if you're meeting his needs alone, and carried on the

A fussy baby can often be
calmed in a baby carrier.

back if his twin needs cuddling or nursing at the same time.
You might try placing both twins in carriers, one in front and
one in back, or both in front. Or put one baby in a front carrier, and you'll still have two arms free to carry his twin.
(This usually works best during the first few months.)

● If both babies are distressed at once, spend a lot of
time in the rocking chair. The rhythm will help to calm you,
as well as the babies.

● Go for a walk outside with the babies, or to an enclosed mall, if it is too cold. It helps to get out of the house
and *move* with your babies!

● Few child-care experts would recommend picking up
and carrying two babies at the same time without one being
in a carrier. (These experts have also not had to listen to two
crying babies every day.) Therefore, it is pointless to tell you
not to do this. When you carry both babies, though, never
forget for one second that you have no way to break a fall. Be
on guard constantly for objects on the floor, and walk slowly.
Sit or put a baby down as soon as possible. Your babies will
practically mold to your body, and you are constantly adapt-
ing to minute changes in their weights and ability to

balance. Unless another person is with you and the babies every day, it is extremely dangerous to allow them to carry both babies at once.

● Bathe in the tub with one baby at a time. (This is a nice way for father to get extra skin contact with his babies, too.) Warm water relaxes everyone. Do not step in or out of a slippery tub with a baby in your arms. Place baby on a towel on the floor before getting out yourself.

● If your babies have difficulty breastfeeding simultaneously, then you may find yourself nursing one while coping with another crying, hungry baby. This is not a relaxing way to breastfeed. *Touch* Baby B while feeding Baby A. You can put the baby in a cradle, buggy, or rocking infant seat, and rock the baby with your feet while feeding the other. You can wrap your feet around the crying baby to establish skin contact until you can feed him. He at least knows you're with him.

Chapter Eight

Coping with Hospitalization

O n rare occasions, a young baby has a problem that requires hospitalization. The mother of twins often feels
torn between comforting the sick baby with her presence,
and meeting the needs of the baby who is well. *Both need the
mother intensely.* If you find yourself with this uncomfortable decision, there are options that can meet the needs of
both babies:

Arrange to take both babies to the hospital. This has
worked well for many mothers of multiples. Some parents
have even changed physicians and/or hospitals in order to
keep the nursing family intact. This idea may be especially
helpful if hospitalization is necessarily many miles from
home.

*The second-best arrangement is to have the well twin
brought to the hospital, or have you go to the well baby
several times a day for feedings and physical contact.* Of
course, this is difficult if the hospital is very far from home.

*When you are the one requiring hospitalization, ask
before admission if the babies could be brought in to*

nurse. Again, parents have changed physicians and/or hospitals to accommodate the need of all to remain in close contact. If hospitalization is a sudden decision, you probably won't have time to consider the options of keeping the nursing trio together. Perhaps, when you finally have time to think, you could ask if the babies can be brought in. Start expressing milk as soon as possible to maintain your needed supply. But even if the milk supply greatly diminishes or seems absent, *frequent nursing,* balanced diet, lots of fluids, and rest will help bring in an adequate amount of milk again when you get home.

Sometimes a close family member must be hospitalized, and your presence is needed. Once again — mothers have taken the babies into the hospital or had the babies brought to the hospital several times each day for feedings and physical contact. If absolutely necessary, you could leave the hospital and go to the babies, but you will soon be exhausted trying to be all things to all people.

Be sure the following equipment is available or take your own; rocking chair (folding lawn chair-type will do), baby carrier, light-weight stroller, disposable diapers. If your twins enjoy sitting in an infant seat, be sure that is there also. (Take extra changes of baby clothes or let both babies wear hospital gowns, eliminating laundry.)

No matter who is hospitalized, the ideal is for mother and babies to remain together for the duration of the hospital stay. This ideal is often attainable, but it will be up to you and your husband to pursue it. As a parent, you not only have the right but the responsibility to see that the needs of your babies are met in the best possible way. The following ideas might also help you to explore your options, no matter who is hospitalized:

☐   Ask your physician if hospital admission is absolutely necessary. *Often* — treatment, tests, or surgery *can* be done on an outpatient basis. If you do not feel comfortable or sure

Breastfeeding is too important to be abandoned because of hospitalization.

of the physician's explanation of the problem and/or treatment, continue to ask questions until you are completely satisfied. Ultimately, you are responsible for your health care and that of your babies, so never feel inhibited about seeking adequate explanations. It is your right.

☐   Explain as many times as required that it is impossible to treat one of a nursing trio without affecting the other two. It can be difficult for health care professionals to understand the intimacy of the breastfeeding relationship, and that you and your babies are in a physical harmony, also. Help them learn that breastfeeding is more than a way of getting food into babies, and that it is the perfect nourishment for healing.

☐   Discuss the need you have for your babies, as well as their need for you. A doctor may be concerned that meeting the needs of two babies during a hospitalization will be too taxing for you. Only you can make him aware that worrying about their welfare, and feeling torn about whose needs are greatest, is a much greater burden for you to carry.

☐   Should you ever be told to wean because of a medical problem or medication you must take, call your La Leche League Leader. She will be able to help you explore alternatives that might be available in your personal situation.

Chapter Nine

Enhancing Individuality

A s a mother of twins, you undoubtedly want to watch each twin grow into a self-confident, self-sufficient adult. At the same time, you want them to enjoy the special relationship that only twins can share as they mature. If this ever makes you feel you are on a tightrope over an alligator pit, you aren't alone! But it is possible to have both. When twins realize their individuality, they are free to enjoy the twin relationship.

Breastfeeding is a wonderful way to begin individualizing your twins. It removes the temptations that could compromise close contact, and it helps you bond with, or get to know, each baby. How can you ever think of them as individuals if you do not get to know each of your infants? Here are some other ideas to help you get acquainted with each twin:

● The bonding period can be influenced by the type of babies you have. Opposite-sex twins are usually regarded as individuals before same-sex twins. It takes more time to get to know identical twins as separate, unique persons, compared to same-sex fraternal twins.

● During the early months, you know you see *two* babies, but it may *seem* you are only caring for one baby who keeps you totally busy. (This is difficult to explain and only another twin mother can understand.)

● Look for differences. There are always differences, no matter how alike the babies may seem. Often one has a fuller face or a different look about the eyes. Look for some type of marking such as a freckle or a birthmark.

● If you cannot yet tell one from another, take extra I.D. bracelets home from the hospital. Paint the fingernail or toenail of one baby. You could initial the bottom of the twin's feet with a non-toxic magic marker. Use different colored diaper pins for each baby, or put iron-on letter transfers on their tee shirts for family or neighborhood gatherings.

● Go out of your way to call each baby by name during feedings, diaper changes, or while cuddling them. While you can't expect the lady up the street or the grocery clerk to remember one from the other, encourage relatives, friends, and close neighbors to call them by name. Discourage those who frequently refer to them as *twin, twinnie,* or *the twins,* especially in their presence. (Never admit to anyone that you have difficulty telling them apart in front of the twins. Can you imagine how you would feel if your parents weren't sure who *you* were?)

● Take pictures of each baby alone, as well as pictures of them together.

Though twins may appear identical, their mother should find a way to tell them apart.

● If you find yourself dressing them alike, don't worry about it until your twins have reached an age when they could be choosing their own clothing each morning (usually between three to six years of age). If so compelled, try dressing them in the same outfit, but each in a different color. This "color coding" has the added benefit of identifying one from the other. As an example, for most male twins there will be one blue outfit. Put the same twin in blue and people will soon learn to call him by name (according to the color he wears). The other twin wears another color and is identified by process of elimination.

● Don't label the babies. For example, "Baby A" is the extrovert and "Baby B" is the introvert. It's unfair to be categorized, and twins often *alternate* personality traits. They can *switch dominance,* too.

Iron-on names can identify the twins at family gatherings.

● You will probably find one baby is fussier and demands more of your time. It is not unusual to feel closer, at an earlier date, to the fussier twin — because of the extra contact. You may feel guilty because you are not paying as much attention to the more patient baby. Of course, you will want to try to give any extra time to your patient twin — but try not to feel guilty if you cannot. The patient baby will eventually demand equal time when he needs it, by switching personality traits briefly; often, he will become the toddler who will need you more!

● If you are out with one twin and someone remarks about your adorable child (and he's old enough to understand), avoid the temptation to reveal the existence of the similar adorable child you have. (This is more difficult than it sounds!) This twin is listening to your response. (Always announcing his twinness might make him feel his twinness has more value to you than his uniqueness.)

● Be on guard against letting your ego interfere with your twin's individuality. You become a celebrity by default, simply by giving birth to twins. This may tempt you to reinforce the idea of them as a unit. It is normal for your ego to inflate a bit with this celebrity status, so don't feel guilty about it. Just don't let it get in the way of each child's individual needs.

● Stop and think, "If these children were a year apart, would I be so worried about treating them exactly the same at all times?" — when worrying about spending equal time with each twin.

When each twin knows you consider him special in his own right, there will be no difficulty with the concept of individuality for the twins, or for you, either!

Don't look on the twins as a unit; remember they are separate individuals.

Chapter Ten

Streamlined Housekeeping

A s a mother of twins, you will become efficient because there is no other choice! Time will be at a premium for quite awhile. One mother of multiples expressed it this way, "It's as if you used to have a whole shipload of time, but now you're in a small lifeboat. You have to throw everything overboard that there isn't room for."

You needn't be a Super Mom! However, in order to meet your twins' needs and those of the rest of your family, *it is necessary to set priorities*. What really *must* be done? Since the babies cannot be expected to compromise their needs, caring for them is *top* priority. Other family members are *second* priority. Your family will need to eat, and clean clothes are always nice. Beyond this, *nothing* is essential. Don't forget your own needs. Hopefully, the following suggestions will add time to spend with your family:

Have full-time household help, if possible, when you bring the twins home. It is unrealistic to think you can meet the babies' needs and those of other family members, plus recover from the delivery, without help. A husband who can take vacation time, a relative, social service agency, or senior citizen center are possible prospects. Honestly evaluate your prospective helper's ability to fulfill the household needs, so you are free to get to know your babies and increase your milk supply with frequent nursings. (The two go together so well.) Let your helper know in advance that the duties will be physical care of older children, cooking, laundry, cleaning, etc. Inform the helper that you are breastfeeding the twins, and only *positive* comments are appreciated!

Limit visitors the first weeks, and let them know you are not worried about being the perfect hostess. If you feel you must offer a snack, direct your company to the proper spot in the kitchen. Remind them to pour you something to drink and bring you a snack, too. Hang a sign on the door that could read, "Babies and Mom are napping. Call at 3:00 p.m. to see if we're having a good day for company," to discourage drop-ins. Be frank with guests if you are tired and feel you must cut their visit short.

There are many ways to cut corners on routine baby care. Diaper service or paper diapers, at least for the first couple of months, can be a tremendous help. Since newborn twins use approximately 180 diapers a week, you would be laundering them almost daily. It costs very little extra for double diaper service, and this help pays off in extra time for family and yourself. If you do your own diapers, buy them prefolded. Leave them in a basket or drawer, until you're ready to change a baby. Have diapers and a pail available at any level of the house where babies may be changed. Double-diaper, especially at night. You can change the babies assembly-line style on the floor, using small waterproof sheeting. Make diaper-changing a play time for reinforcing each baby's name and exercising their arms and legs.

Borrow as much baby clothing as possible, so you can wash it less often. (Lender should mark her initial on all clothing.) You can buy and sell clothing for twins and siblings at reasonable prices as a member of a Mothers of Twins

Taking time to relax with your babies is more important than cleaning the house.

Club. Most groups have clothing sales once or twice a year. Unless a baby has very sensitive skin, place baby laundry in with family loads.

Most babies do not get so dirty that they need a daily bath. If you keep the diaper area clean and each face wiped off, your twins will probably do nicely with a weekly bath. Some babies find a warm bath so relaxing that they will sleep extra long. If this is the case, you might bathe them more often!

To aid meal preparation, collect recipes that can be prepared in stages. Casseroles are a good example because meat can be thawing while vegetables are chopped. The meat can be cooked and added later in the day. Throw in a can of soup and voila! Household appliances like crockpots and pressure cookers can save considerable time. You may find a microwave oven helpful.

A grocery store that delivers may charge a bit more, but you will probably save money since impulse buying is minimized. A milkman not only delivers milk, but many can also bring eggs, yogurt, and cheese to your door. Find out the type of stores on your husband's route to his job so he can make quick stops before coming home, or ask him to take over grocery shopping.

Plan one night out of the kitchen a week. Go to a restaurant where nutritious food is served and babies are welcome. Have your husband call home early in the day to see how things are going at home. Perhaps he could pick up supper on his way home from work or call out for a pizza, if it's been a hectic day. You can relax knowing you won't have to worry about meal preparation.

If friends ask how they can help, tell them to bring a meal after the excitement dies down, or your help returns home. Suggest that these meals be delivered in containers that need not be returned, to make it even easier on you. If they prepare the meal in your kitchen, you will have the pleasure of their company, and perhaps a few extra arms to help with the babies as well. A friend who will sometimes do grocery shopping relieves you of a great responsibility.

Be a catalog shopper for the next few years. Do your holiday gift buying from your living room. Reasonably priced, well-constructed children's clothing is at your fingertips if you order from major department stores known for catalog sales. If you begin using mail order service, you will soon be receiving special sale catalogs, also.

Cut housework to a minimum. You can't do everything, so you will have to make choices. The housework will always be there, but your babies will not be babies for long. Use laundry baskets to collect the clutter, and put it away at your convenience. Read labels for laundry care before you buy clothing to minimize ironing. Even preschoolers can put laundry away, if it has been placed in individual boxes after folding. Clean the bathroom after taking a shower, when everything is already steamy, by wiping with your damp towel. Put dirty dishes in the sink and fill it with hot, soapy water for soaking. The kitchen will appear cleaner when counter tops are empty, and you can wash dishes when time

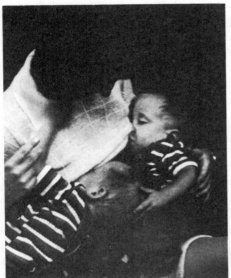

Older babies can easily position themselves for nursing and often touch and caress each other as they nurse together.

allows. Use paper plates and cups and throw the mess away. Within your budget, do or buy anything that simplifies household duties and allows more time to enjoy your family and yourself.

Many mothers of twins continue having weekly household help for several months. A high school or college student will often do housecleaning at reasonable rates. Other mothers have daily help with babies and older children during meal preparation times. Call your local high school guidance counselor for possible names.

Diaper service, household help, grocery delivery, etc., may seem extravagant when two babies are already straining family finances. However, these things will save literally hundreds of extra hours to spend with the people in your family. When you are breastfeeding twins, the money savings can be substantial. You can rationalize a lot of spending by breastfeeding!

Chapter Eleven

What You'll Need

T here are different types of infant equipment that can really make life easier for the mother of twins. It might be possible to borrow some — or locate others at garage sales or Mothers of Twins Clubs' sales. It gets rather expensive buying duplicate equipment. (Financial stress is undeniably a problem. You must weigh diaper service vs. washing for two, etc. Discuss these matters openly with your husband until you both feel comfortable with the decisions.)

☐ **As a mother of twins, you might find it helpful to have a rocking chair on every level of your home.** A good rocker will hold you and your twins for years. You may find you *live* in it for at least the first six months! Your favorite rocker should be where you spend most of your time. Also, you could use one or more folding lawn chair-type rockers in the other areas of the house, and for traveling or visiting with someone. Rocking not only soothes the babies, but the rhythm will also soothe a fussy mother or sibling. Never be without a rocking chair! (It should be tax deductible for mothers of twins!)

☐   **Baby carriers can be very useful.** Try to have two available. If your twins are in different routines, you can carry one baby and get things done around the house. If the baby falls asleep, put him to bed in the carrier so you don't disturb his sleep. You can put a carrier on your back so you can hold or feed the other twin in front. You might even be able to carry two babies at once and still have your hands free. Try placing one in front and one on your back, or carry both babies in front. Twins, especially, cannot receive *too much* close contact. Baby carriers offer this, plus two free hands. Be sure to get well-constructed carriers that can be worn front or back and offer good head support for young babies.

☐   **You will probably find the purchase of a twin stroller an absolute must.** Twins often use a stroller longer than other children because it is not practical to chase after two toddlers running in different directions! A good stroller is worth the investment. A side-by-side double stroller or buggy can be useful for long walks; however, many mothers find

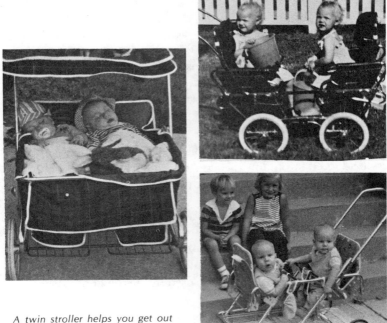

A twin stroller helps you get out with both babies.

them too big and bulky. They are difficult to handle without help and are too wide to pass through some doors. In a limousine-type twin stroller, babies face each other. The seats adjust to a flat position for younger babies. This stroller is easily handled and is as narrow as a standard stroller. One disadvantage is that older babies and toddler twins face each other and fight. Also, there is little leg room for older toddlers. If you have a toddler in additon to twins, an extra front-facing seat is available to attach to the limousine-type stroller's handlebars and goes behind the front-facing twin. (See Appendix.) You may find two umbrella-type strollers, hooked together, meet your needs. But do get them with swivel wheels, and obtain steel clamps to put the two together. It is compact and portable. Together, they are narrow enough to pass through most doors, and you have a single stroller when you want it. Although it is generally less expensive to buy two of these strollers initially, you may find them less durable, necessitating the purchase of two *more* before your babies outgrow them. (Other types of twin strollers are available in other countries.) When purchasing what may seem like an expensive item, keep in mind the number of years you will use it, and the resale value it will have.

☐   **Government-approved car safety seats are absolute necessities.** Do not scrimp in this area. Invest in ones that can be adapted for infants through preschool age. The initial expense may be higher, but in the long run this will save you money.

☐   **Rather than invest in a bulky, four-foot square playpen, you might find a *porta-yard* (Kiddy Korral) or the "Crawl Space" more useful. (Now square with vertical slats.)** These play yards can be used inside the home, as well as out of doors, and they fold much smaller for travel than an ordinary playpen. It is also less expensive. Although not as

Porta-yards can be used outdoors to keep twins in one place.

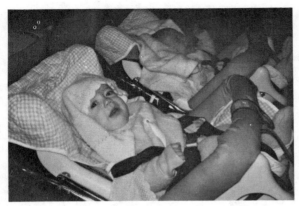

Two car seats are essential equipment.

pretty as most playpens, it allows the babies much more freedom of movement. Most twins can use this porta-yard well into the second or third year. (Even though the twins may seem relatively safe in the play-yard, you still need to remain in hearing within sight of the babies.)

☐ **Automatic swings can be a great help when feeding one baby, or meeting the needs of other children.** One can be enough, but you might borrow another, if you have enough room or live in a two-story home.

☐ **Until the babies are several months old, one crib (or none) is all you need.** The babies have been in close contact within you for many months, and they often sleep more soundly if allowed to snuggle together in a single crib or your bed. Between three to six months, twins may begin disturbing each other, making two cribs a necessity.

Using a family bed can be less convenient with two babies; however, it is not impossible. A king-size bed will give you needed room. You could also take the side railing off a crib and lower the mattress to the level of your mattress, pushing it next to your bed, and fastening it securely.

☐ **There are many baby products on the market that sound wonderful, but you and your babies could live**

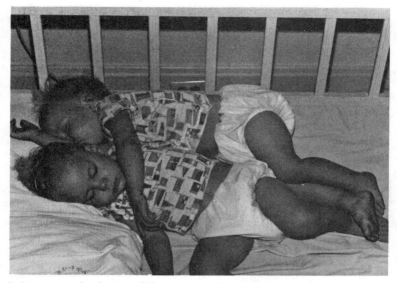

Twins may need only one crib for many months.

without them. A changing table is nice, but a waterproof pad on the rug will work just as well, allowing you to change both at once. There is no worry of a baby falling, either. Infant tubs for baths are fine, but there are alternatives that are less expensive. You could put each baby in an infant seat in the adult tub for baths, or bathe babies, one at a time, with you or your husband. You would be well-advised to do without special towels, soaps, detergents, lotions, potions, etc. Babies have such a nice scent of their own, why spoil it and spoil their skin? When your twins are several months old, you may be tempted to let the babies get around in walkers. It might seem that these would give you a break while babies explore on their own. But babies in walkers must be watched *constantly*, to ensure they don't tip over or go down the stairs. Also, walkers could impede the babies' physical and mental development, since they need to be on the floor to learn to move their bodies without props. Some babies can reach objects while in a walker that would otherwise have taken months to discover. This can be dangerous. Why rush it?

☐   **As your babies get older, other equipment will come in handy.** You will need two high chairs or sassy seats. Pressure gates or expandable indoor gates will be very helpful once your babies start crawling. These can keep them either in or out of a certain room. Curious creepers need a gate at stairways, too. When the twins start standing and climbing, shoulder harnesses for use in the stroller seats and high chairs will prevent many worry lines for you!

Much of this equipment is beneficial as long as you keep the purpose of it in mind. Equipment is meant to *help* you — not replace you! When meeting the needs of two babies plus other family members, it is so easy to abuse something that gives you a break. But porta-yards, automatic swings, infant seats, etc., cannot replace your arms. Your babies *need* your touch. A rocking chair is better than an automatic swing because it includes *you*. A twin can be just as safe in a porta-yard as in a baby carrier, *but* in the carrier he is seeing more of the world (and has body contact with you) at the same time. Also, twins have the same need to explore the environment as singletons, but it is more difficult to monitor *two* babies discovering the world. It is understandable that you might want to contain their enthusiasm in a porta-yard some of the time, but it is unfair to suppress the babies' natural need to investigate their surroundings. Porta-yards are helpful in protecting the babies from older children, or while you are busy elsewhere in the house, but constant use is abuse. The use of doorway gates will allow a much larger area for exploration.

Chapter Twelve

Out and About

I t is much more complicated to get up and go with twins than it is with a single baby. It may take so long to prepare for an excursion that you feel too tired to leave when finally ready! When you must go out without another adult to help you with the babies, you may feel scared to leave. You might wonder what you'd do if both babies started to cry while the three of you are out.

But it is important to get up and out of the house. Even a twenty-minute stroll can help put things in perspective. It's worth the effort to go for a walk outside, or to an enclosed shopping mall, when taking care of two babies becomes overwhelming. So many people will come up and comment on how sweet your twins are that you will start believing it again! The following are some ideas for coordinating the whole affair:

Place each baby in the seat of a twin stroller. If the seats are in a flat position, and your young infants become startled or cry every time you hit a bump in the pavement, secure each baby in a narrow, inexpensive infant seat. Place the infant seat with baby in the flattened stroller seat. Put the stroller seatbelt around the infant seat and stroller seat, or you can use pillows to make babies feel more secure, less wobbly. If you have a toddler or preschooler, he could ride on the middle bar of a limousine-type stroller.

Put one baby in a single stroller and let one ride in a baby carrier. Unless one baby has a strong preference for stroller or carrier, alternate which baby gets close contact in the carrier. Going out this way is useful when you don't have the time or desire to attract attention. Most people won't notice your twins until you've passed them. Another option is to wear one baby in a carrier, have one baby in a twin stroller seat, and a toddler in the other stroller seat. The older child usually loves this.

It is virtually impossible to shop for yourself with two babies along. So take along a mother's helper. Or if your husband is walking or shopping with you, then both could use a baby carrier or push single strollers.

Taking both babies to the grocery store isn't easy.

If for some reason you must do grocery shopping alone, try placing one twin in a baby carrier and the other in a narrow, inexpensive infant seat. Put the infant seat in the space designed for a child to sit in the shopping cart. As the babies get older, wear a carrier with one twin on your back and let the other twin ride in the shopping cart seat. When they are too heavy for any type of carrier, put each in the seat of a shopping cart. Push one cart and pull the other. It may be a good idea to have the babies secured in the shopping cart with shoulder harnesses. If both twins are allowed to stand in one shopping cart, they can easily tip it over, if both rush to the narrow end. *Never leave a child alone for a moment in a shopping cart.*

If you ever needed an excuse for being late, you really have it now. Keep a diaper bag ready to go at all times. It could contain diapers, plastic pants, plastic bags, a waterproof pad, extra diaper pins, disposable wash cloths, an extra change of clothes, and a baby food grinder or nonperishable snacks for older babies.

If you must be somewhere in the morning, dress them in their traveling clothes the night before. If you use triple diapers at night, you may be able to wait until you reach your destination to change them in the morning.

When scheduling appointments you must keep with the babies, e.g., doctor's visits, ask to be given a time that requires minimum waiting. When possible, bring along Daddy, Grandma, or mother's helper to help you with the babies. If you must go alone, call ahead to see if you can bring your twin stroller inside. After explaining that you will be coming with two babies, most places are very understanding and willing to oblige. (But why is it no matter how prepared you seem, the twins will each manage to have a large bowel movement the moment you fasten the seat belts of their car seats!?)

You might want to keep a baby carrier where the twins

Two baby carriers can be worn in front when twins are small.

sleep so it would be possible to carry both in case of fire, especially if your husband works at night or there are other small children in the family. A carrier always kept in the car could be a lifesaver should you have a breakdown or run out of gas. Hopefully, you will never experience these problems, but you might worry less if you feel more prepared.

Chapter Thirteen

Brothers and Sisters

T he birth of twins can be difficult emotionally for other children in your family. Not only are you occupied with a twenty-four hour job, but siblings soon learn that twins are celebrities, attracting attention wherever they go. Sisters and brothers are often totally ignored by others.

In addition to taking up most of your day, the babies are probably waking for night feedings so you are not getting much rest. Lack of sleep can lead to a build-up of tension. Everyday occurrences that used to be annoying may now loom as major catastrophes. For example, spilled milk is usually a minor aggravation, but when coping with two babies plus preschoolers, it may produce near-hysteria. Sometimes you may feel that you can't cope with one more thing to do.

You and your older children will survive. You will have more time for all your children as months go by. Here are ideas that might help during the intense infancy period.

Five minutes of your time when a child *needs* it, will be more beneficial than an hour when it is more convenient for you. There can be time for hugs and kisses even when you can't sit and hold each for a long period. Touch each one, give each a brief backrub at night. Say over and over, "I love you."

Weekend vacations at grandparents, special friends, or relatives can give the sibling time to be the center of attention, while you have fewer responsibilities for one or two days. Even visiting for supper or overnight may be a break for everyone. These things should only be done if the child is old enough and does not view this as being shut out.

Ask a friend or babysitter to stay during the babies' naps, so you can take the older children somewhere special. This may be a trip to the zoo or just a walk around the block, if naps or calm times are very brief. Take advantage of this time to talk. Or you could have a friend take the twins for a walk so you can read a story or sit in the rocker with an older child without interruptions.

Remind your children that you are aware of their adjustments. Let them know you are available to listen.

Talk to your children about your feelings. Tell them that you sometimes feel overwhelmed. Even a young child can understand the emotion, if not the words. Say this often as young children easily forget. Don't be afraid to cry in front of your children, if that is what you feel like doing. Talking about feeling overwhelmed and crying often go hand-in-hand!

Children are sometimes jealous of a new sibling. When they must bond and cope with *two* new siblings, it is understandable that jealous behavior might be exaggerated. Regressive behavior, like wetting pants after toilet learning, is not uncommon. Who wouldn't want to be a baby with all the attention the twins are getting? Try to keep calm and not punish regressive behavior. Older children may release tension with outbursts of anger, thumb-sucking, nail-biting, etc. Some children go out of their way to find mischief while you breastfeed the babies. Usually physical contact, reminders that they are loved, and the passage of time will lessen these problems.

Remind visitors that older children are going through a period of adjustment. (Ask them ahead of time to notice the older children first.)

Whether asked or not, bring attention to the older children when out in public, if someone notices the twins. You can tell people all the children's names, ages, interests, etc. (Remind your older children that twins are noticed because they are different.)

Avoid emphasizing your babies' twinness by bringing attention to them as a unit. Guard against letting your ego hurt your children. If you buy iron-on transfers to put names on each baby's tee-shirt, offer to do the same for all siblings, but use only for family or neighborhood gatherings. When taking pictures of the twins, be sure to include brothers and

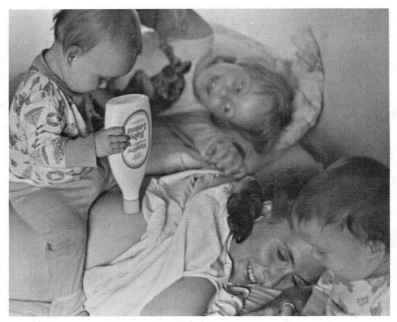

Mom gets a few minutes of rest while babies romp on the bed.

sisters in part of a photography session. All children in the family are special.

Discourage the family being divided into "the twins" and "all the other children." Within reason, let the babies be held and cuddled by siblings. (Why, oh why, do big brothers and sisters always want to hug, kiss, and cuddle the new family member when the babies are finally fast asleep, and you have a moment's peace?) Involve older children in the babies' care by fetching diapers, getting a snack for you while nursing, or telling one baby, "Mommy is coming soon," while you are busy with the other.

Down-play the fact that family outings may occur infrequently for a while. It is harder to get up and go when there is more than one baby, and older children will resent the babies if you blame the twins for this curtailment of social activities.

Take out the photo albums and baby books. Talk about each child's infancy. Tell them how you met their needs and how much time it took. Remind them that this time *two* babies need you. Each needs you as much as a single child. If you do this during nursings, some mischief may be avoided.

Father is indispensable when caring for the other children. He can give individual time and attention to each child, and *you* time alone with your babies.

Dad can take the twins out for a walk to give mom a break.

Chapter Fourteen

Husband and Wife

T he birth of twins always requires more adjustment in a marriage than the birth of a singleton. The support and encouragement of your husband is more important than anything else when breastfeeding, caring for other children, or explaining how supper didn't get cooked again!

It is so important to keep lines of communication open. Here are ideas that other parents of multiples have found helpful:

You need time together as a couple. But when meeting the needs of infant twins, it can be difficult to find even five minutes in a day for talking with one another. A family walk keeps all children busy, and you and your husband can enjoy a relaxed conversation. Try to plan a "nice" dinner at home once a week. Hamburger by candlelight can seem romantic, even when you are each holding a baby. Let good friends know that you, your husband, and babies will be free to visit almost anytime. Or invite them over to your house for a meal while the twins are young and your social activities must be

curtailed. (If you let them know the cuisine will be simple, due to the babies' demands, they are likely to offer to bring at least one course!)

If you or your husband feel you must have time alone together, keep in mind babies' need for your presence. Try to go out only during the twins' nap, or, if possible, after bedtime. If your babies don't take naps at the same time or go to bed early enough, leave briefly only during calm times after a relaxed feeding. Even an hour at a nearby restaurant can be enough time alone to feel refreshed. If you and your husband do leave the babies briefly, be sure the sitter is mature enough to handle two babies. You might consider having two people (one to care for each twin). Remind babysitters that you will be gone just a short time, so babies will not need anything to eat until you arrive home. (You could leave two small bottles of expressed breast milk in the refrigerator just in case.)

Ask your husband what he most likes to see accomplished around the house. Go out of your way to do one special thing a day for him. Try to get household help, if a spotless home is really important to him. Even if you only get one thing done all day, try to make *his* request that one thing.

Let your husband know how overwhelmed you sometimes feel. Twins can seem more like quadruple work than double work. (Fortunately, they can also bring quadruple joy.) One of the advantages of twins is that it is almost impossible for a husband not to get involved with caring for babies.

Keep in mind the adjustments your husband must make with the birth of twins. Not only is his lovely and adoring wife busy caring for babies twenty-four hours a day, but he may feel a very real extra financial burden providing for this baby bonanza! "Two for the price of one" does not cover twins.

Most couples are told to curtail sexual intercourse during the last months of a multiple pregnancy. Now that the babies are born, there is no physical reason for not making love. But you may find your interest in sexual relations hits an all-time low. Whether it's due to hormonal influences, fatigue, not wanting to be touched by one more person that

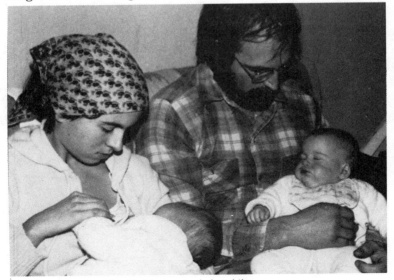

One down, one to go. Dad holds sleeping baby while mom nurses the other one.

day, or a combination, isn't really important. A patient and understanding husband is important, and you both need to realize that things will improve as the babies get older.

To make the most of marital relations, find time when you are not too tired. You'll feel more relaxed if babies are sleeping or during their calm times. Involve older children in a long project. (Isn't this why "Sesame Street" is on television?) Say to your husband sometime, "I've got ten minutes free, meet you in our bedroom in two minutes—be ready!" He knows what you mean, and he *will* be! Given the choice between seeing the house cleaned or love-making, his decision will probably not be difficult to make. Let your husband know that sometimes it is enough for you to be held, kissed, and told how much you are loved. Communicate about your sexual needs and encourage him to be honest with you about his needs. When you want to satisfy his sexual needs quickly, approach him in a physical rather than emotional way. Say, "I want *you*," rather than "I want to make love." Speak graphically of his body. (Use your imagination!) Even though you may not be able to tell him how you love him in a physical way as often, tell him often that you love him and appreciate his understanding.

Though you may not have been built like Racquel Welch prior to your twin pregnancy, if your abdominal skin looks like seersucker afterwards, you may feel self-conscious. Tell your husband if you feel less sexually attractive due to your "twin skin"; it will probably bother you more than it bothers him.

Together, coping with the stress that twins seem to impose on a marriage can really enhance a good relationship with mutual growth. You will appreciate each other much more for the sacrifices made and maturity displayed.

Chapter Fifteen

Other Mothers Say

T he best way to understand what it's like to have twins is to hear what other mothers of twins say about their experience. The following stories are taken from LLL NEWS.

Nursing Twins
by Patricia Berg, New York

I had nursed two children previously when we discovered we were expecting twins, so I had no doubts as to whether I'd have "enough milk." I was, however, very anxious to leave the hospital with the babies as soon after delivery as possible if all went well.

Our girls, Joelle and Megan, arrived in December weighing five pounds thirteen ounces and six pounds. They were taken immediately to the nursery and I stared at the ceiling for six hours until they were brought to me. We then enjoyed total rooming-in until we went home twenty-four hours later.

My husband, Ted, took time off work when I returned home. We spent a wonderfully peaceful vacation with our children. We didn't hire someone to come in after Ted returned to work. In retrospect I think it would have been helpful to have a high school girl come for a few hours a day to help with my two older children (then five and three) and do light housework.

Those first weeks were tiring but a patient husband who was willing to rock and soothe a fussy baby made it much easier. I got to know Megan very quickly since she slept little and needed a great deal of nursing and contact. My relationship with Joelle was a little slower in forming as she was quieter and it seemed we had less time together in the beginning.

I realize now that I often hesitated to nurse the girls simultaneously during those early weeks. However, when I did nurse them together (their feet toward my back, heads on a pillow), I found that the rush of good feelings so familiar to the nursing mother came even more easily. There's just something about four little eyes looking up at you so absorbingly. I also found that nursing the babies together would bring on a very strong let-down whenever I felt my supply a little low, usually late in the afternoon.

I was fortunate to have a baby carrier and borrowed another one. I strongly recommend a good carrier that will support a newborn's head even when worn on the back. This leaves your front available for nursing. I was also known to carry the babies one on my front, one on my back on occasion. I've been able to get out frequently carrying Meg in the baby carrier and Jo in a stroller. We've attracted a lot of attention and met a lot of nice people this way. I had intended to switch the babies letting Jo ride in the carrier some of the time, but Meg would fuss so when carried any other way. I feel this was due to her apparent need for so much more contact in those early weeks.

My advice to anyone expecting twins would be to keep in mind that the needs of a twin do not diminish by half because there are two babies. Each baby still needs lots of sucking, closeness, and responsiveness from a loving family. The need for your babies to be with you is the same as for a single infant. They cannot "comfort" each other until much later and it's still mom they zero in on to feel safe and secure.

Resign yourself to spending most of your time caring for babies that first year. It's time well spent fostering the ties that will help you over the rough spots.

Key in on your favorite people and spend lots of time with them visiting and having them over. Good friends can be wonderfully helpful and people seem to automatically respond to your need for an "extra" hand. (I've had perfect strangers help me out many times when shopping, etc.)

Remember to call on the League when you have questions or doubts. They can put you in touch with someone who's been through it.

Finally, savor the experience of nursing your twins. It is unique and immensely gratifying. Happy baby times two!

Reprinted from La Leche League NEWS, March-April 1979.

Nursing My Twins
by Patti Lemberg, Texas

When I first told my husband that I planned to nurse our expected child, he hit the ceiling with an emphatic NO. Our doctor, however, was glad and suggested that I attend La Leche League meetings for the education and moral support. She also suggested that Mac and I attend classes in prepared childbirth, which we did. I shared my LLL reading material with Mac, and by the time we learned we were expecting twins, he was convinced that prepared childbirth and nursing were "the only way."

So we were all ready when the boys were born. Due to a little too much "help," a little too little privacy, and a lot too little time allowed with each child, they didn't nurse well in the hospital. But once home they settled in my arms and began nursing like real champs.

They nursed about every two hours for twenty minutes at a time and slept one four or five-hour stretch a day. The hardest time for me was the six-week growth spurt, when each of them nursed every forty-five mintues. It was a bit much, but I just took the same attitude I had taken during the last weeks of pregnancy: "Next year this time they'll be toddling around, so cute — I won't even remember this day." I did have sore nipples, but I put the least hungry twin on the most sore breast. It only hurt for about two minutes while they were just getting started, and my breast healed soon.

The mothers in my League Group helped me enjoy my babies with their relaxed, patient attitude. I had been raised "never to leave the house with dirty dishes in the sink," but I learned to do this — and more! The first two months we had diaper service; we used the playpen for a clean laundry depot for the first four months; Mac took over the shopping duties for the first year, and so on. Our priority list: babies, Mom, Dad, food, laundry, with house cleaning bringing up the rear. (Mac really felt as if he was first because he had a happy wife and healthy, happy babies.)

By two and half months the boys had settled back to nursing every two to three hours and twice each during the night. (Six hours equals a "night" for a wee one.) The only problem was that David was an early bird and Alan was a night owl.

Between six and seven months, both voted to adopt a four-hour schedule, and I promptly donated fifty ounces of milk in a week's time. But this, too, passed, and now at seventeen months they usually nurse only at sleep-related times.

The question I get most often is how I position them for simultaneous nursings. When they were tiny each rested in the crook of an arm, bottom at my hand, legs extended along my thigh. If one wriggled out of place I caught the back of the diaper and pulled him back. In fact, I still use this position if they both want to rock and nurse at the same time. Another good position is sitting on the couch with heads in lap and bodies extended under my arms onto the couch. This one is great because both hands are free to hold a book and sip a beverage. When they are still tiny it's best to put a pillow under each for height and comfort. These days, we prefer to nurse lying down on their bed (a mattress on the floor), with David on the left in the standard nursing positon for lying down and Alan on the right across my chest. That may sound awkward, but any position that is comfortable to all is fine. You need to work with the furniture and pillows until you find what's best for you.

The most valuable piece of furniture I owned during the first six months was a big overstuffed rocking chair my Dad bought at a garage sale.

The most important advantage I have gleaned from the whole nursing experience is confidence. I know my way of mothering is good, and that makes me happy, which in turn relaxes me into a patient frame of mind, which can't help but increase my intuitiveness, which induces loving guidance rather than instant hysteria, fostering positive results which breed pride and confidence! It's a lovely merry-go-round. Now, with two toddlers running in and out, complete with sand and soil, it only takes me about three hours to clean house — including stops for getting drinks, kissing bumps, and loads of "help." When you're on the confidence-patience-relaxation-pride merry-go-round, it will all seem simple!

I'll tack on some helpful hints that occur to me.

- Remember that nursing twins is 90 percent confidence and 10 percent patience.
- Basic advice: nurse whoever is hungry on whichever breast is most full.
- Enjoy your experience with twins from the very beginning by planning for rooming-in during your hospital stay. Rather then being relieved of the "burden" of twins during this time, you need these special hours of contact with YOUR babies to bolster your confidence. When babies are near, you can comfort each as he needs. A baby nurses better if he isn't thwarted by schedules. A mother rests easier if she isn't separated from the little lives that have been and will be for some time so totally dependent on her. Changing and bathing, even two, are not great tasks and are easier learned by the new mother now rather than later.

In the hospital you have help at your fingertips and this arrangement (rooming-in) is less taxing on the nursing staff's time than caring for both babies each day plus bringing them to you on a truly demand schedule. Of course rooming-in isn't possible if your twins are in a special nursery or need special care. But you can visit the nursery and ask to be allowed to hold each of them and possibly even nurse them there.

- Babies do make "sounds." Don't be afraid of one disturbing the other. They may at first, but they need to get used to these and other "household" noises. Everyone will be more comfortable with this relaxed attitude. If you let them share the same crib for about the first five months or so they will probably enjoy the closeness and rest easier.

- A large oval laundry basket with a king-size pillow inside makes a dandy duo caddy at first.

- When things start to pile up and make you tense, bundle up the twins in the stroller and take a walk around the block. If you don't already know your neighbors, keep walking—someone will soon be out to adore your twins. Or you can just sit with the twins in the front yard on a quilt.

- At three or four months of age the task of caring for twins may begin to seem overwhelming because they want constant, individual attention. At this stage they want desperately to move but do not yet have the motor coordination to do so. Try to find a nice grandmotherly neighbor, friend, high school girl, relative, or whatever, to come for a couple of hours every day and just play with one while you play with the other. You can trade periodically. Help them exercise their muscles by holding little hands and pulling up to standing position in your lap. Sing, talk, rock. If you are totally alone, sit on the floor on a quilt or rug and just play with both.

- Be sure to share with your husband all of your ideas, opinions, precious moments, worries, doubts, and be sure to ask him about his. Find out his priorities and try to do something special for him each day. You'll be surprised how much more tolerant and helpful he will be.

- If the kitchen is a disaster area and must be tackled, clean the counters and floor first. If you tire before you reach the dishes, stop and rest. You'll always manage to wash them before you use them again, and you'll feel better if the room is clean.

• When cooking a casserole, make double the recipe and freeze one.

• Make a couple of carbon copies of letters to grandparents and other doting relatives so you don't have to write a separate letter to each one. Keep a diary at bedside and jot down little remembrances each night. Then you can write one great letter (with carbons) a month instead of those weekly "I cleaned house today" and "we had chicken for dinner Tuesday night" notes that are so depressing because you KNOW your life is more involved and special. A little later, when the kids are more independent, use your carbon copies to fill out the baby books.

• Try to overcome your intimidation about nursing your babies in public. True, simultaneous nursings require privacy, but when you're in public, there's always ample help to entertain one while the other is dining. A buttoned blouse could be unbuttoned from the bottom halfway up. The wide lifted part conceals the upper part of the breast and forms a hood over baby's head. Baby covers your tummy. A loose pullover is even better. Separates make ideal nursing attire. A diaper or receiving blanket draped casually over baby provides a cozy secluded spot. A cap with a brim for baby is even better.

• Remember that almost everyone has deep convictions about child rearing and will advise and correct you freely. Reread THE WOMANLY ART OF BREASTFEEDING and Sheila Kippley's *Breastfeeding and Natural Child Spacing* (which is really about a comfortable, enjoyable, relaxed attitude towards mothering as much as about child spacing), and be confident in the understanding of why you feel the way you do. Then you will be able to meet criticism with calm conversation rather than defensiveness.

• Twins, like most nursing babies, have growth spurts around ages six weeks and three months. At these times they really need to nurse more often and in doing so they stimulate an increase in your milk production.

At six weeks you are usually increasing your activities and may tend to forget your own nutritional and sleep needs. Don't! You need to remember that the best way to gauge the amount of input is by the amount of output. You need to remember also that this spurt probably won't last any longer than a week. Fears of "milk dried up" and "no end in sight — tyranny of twins — loss of personal freedom," so common at this time, have no real foundations; ignore them.

The three-month spurt meets you at a calmer moment, but your first thought may be "solids?" You need to remember that the whole purpose of this spurt is to increase your milk supply, and this purpose would be defeated by supplements or introduction of solids at this time.

Babies may also show an increased interest in nursing after solids are introduced. This may be responsible for many abrupt weanings if mothers don't understand what is going on. You need to relax and remember that your babies still need the nutritional benefits of your milk. It may also serve as a confirmation to them that this new stuff in the spoon isn't a replacement for but rather an addition to the milk that comes with the comfort, warmth, and support of mother's arms and breast.

Reprinted from La Leche League NEWS, September-October 1976.

Two Happy Babies
by Lorraine Weisman, Ohio

I had expected to breastfeed my first baby: what I had not expected was twins. I found that what is good for one is better for two! I got some helpful hints from another LLL mother who was nursing twins, and after a slow start we became an efficient nursing threesome.

Paul and Brian each has his own personal time with Mom for eating, playing, and loving. I feel this is really important and don't go along with the athletic feat of feeding the two of them together (except in emergencies when the little guys wake up at the same time). They established a roughly three-hour feeding schedule themselves.

At nearly six months they are sleeping through the night and nursing for much shorter periods. We are beginning to experiment with solids, and they enjoy sticking their hands in their mouths with each messy bite — it's delightful!

In spite of the fact that Paul had what was termed "colic" by the doctor until he was four months old, there were never hours of crying in our house. Often just shorter, more frequent feedings and our rocking chair helped him. Many people have commented on how "good" the boys are at home, in stores, and on visits. I believe that it is because they're breastfed, cuddled, and played with a lot — they're just plain happy.

I never worried about their weight gain (and my sons gained slowly though steadily) in spite of the doctor's suggestions for bottled supplements to "get that weight up." They are thriving and growing and, most of all, happy.

I really recommend breastfeeding twins in spite of disbelief and overconcern from relatives and friends. The time you save by avoiding bottles, etc., is well spent playing with your babies. Enjoy! There are twice as many smiles and hugs, and no one expects you to prepare gourmet meals or mow the lawn; after all, you're breastfeeding twins — unbelievable!

Reprinted from La Leche League NEWS, January-February 1977.

Learning to Love
by Carolyn Farrell, Pennsylvania

So much has been said about how a breastfeeding mother teaches her baby to love by the love she gives him. In my case, I think I learned more about loving and feeling and caring than my babies did.

I didn't have a deeply loving relationship with my parents. They weren't bad parents; I just never felt close to them. My older sister was born six years before me and my younger sister was born five years after me. Because of the wide differences in our ages, we never shared a great deal and so never felt close. I don't remember having a close friend during high school or college either. When I talk about a close friend, I mean one who is *more* than compatible, one with whom I could strongly identify, a kindred spirit if you will. My husband always felt that my inability to have strong, deep feelings for another human being was just part of my emotional character. He felt I was a loner.

The birth of my twins aroused no special excitement in me. I brought them home from the hospital anxious to undertake the new experience of raising children, but they seemed like strangers to me at that time. My contact with La Leche League had sold me on the values of breastfeeding and so with LLL's guidance, I proceeded to breastfeed my twins.

It didn't take long. I soon began to experience *intense* feelings of love for the babies. I found it upsetting to be away from them for more than a few hours. Every move they made, every discomfort they felt, every pleasure they had, reverberated in me. I had never experienced feeling this intense, this wonderful, for any human being before.

I became more involved with La Leche League, and before long I found that it was possible for me to have deeply loving adult relationships too. I am relieved to know that I am capable of loving fully. There always was a certain vacuum in my life previous to my involvement with my babies. I am grateful to my babies for helping me to become the fuller, happier human being that I am now.

Reprinted from La Leche League NEWS, July-August 1973.

Appendix

LA LECHE LEAGUE INTERNATIONAL (LLLI)
9616 Minneapolis Avenue
P.O. Box 1209
Franklin Park IL 60131-8209 USA
(312) 455-7730 (or check phone book for local group)

National Mothers of Twin Clubs, Inc.
Executive Office
5402 Amberwood Lane
Rockville MD 20853 USA
301-460-9108 (Check phone book for local group.)

Newsletter for Parents of Multiples
Double Talk
P.O. Box 412
Amelia OH 45102 USA
513-231-6093

Parents of Multiple Births Association
P.O.M.B.A.
283 — 7th Avenue
Lethbridge Alberta Canada T1J 1H6

Center for Study of Multiple Births
333 E. Superior Street — Suite 463-5
Chicago IL 60611 USA
312-266-9093

Twin Baby Carriers

Double Cuddle — *for newborns through toddlers. Wear two babies in front, one back and one front, or as two single carriers (with purchase of extra straps — sold separately).*

> Cuddle Carriers
> 21 Potsdam Road, Unit 61
> Downsview Ontario Canada M3N 1N3
> 416-663-7143

Twin Matey — *for newborns through toddlers. Wear two babies in front, one back and one front, or as two single carriers (with purchase of extra straps — sold separately).*

> Kidpower Unlimited
> 1081 Bloor Street, West, Suite 300
> Toronto Ontario Canada M5H 1M5
> 416-533-3697

Snugli — *for newborns through toddlers. Snugli, Inc. carries a kit that allows you to adapt two regular Snugli carriers into one with one baby in front and one in back. Carriers can still be used individually.*

> Snugli, Inc.
> 1212 Kerr Gulch
> Evergreen CO 80439 USA
> 303-526-0131

Tandem Seat for Stroller

Taylor Tot Products, Inc.
P.O. Box 636
Frankfort KY 40602 USA
502-695-2000

Twin Adapter for Umbrella Stroller

Gerico, Inc.
P.O. Box 33755
Denver CO 80233 USA
303-457-0926

Strollers

Perego Duetto — *see page 73 (top right photo) seats can face each other or both face forward. Available or can be ordered where Perego Strollers are sold. Perego also makes a triplet stroller.*

MacLaren Twin Buggy — *a side-by-side, umbrella-type double stroller. Backrests recline, fits through doors, folds easily, and is very compact.*

> Andrews MacLaren, Inc.
> P.O. Box 2004
> New York, NY 10017 USA
> 800-233-1224
> (in New York 212-889-7547)

Porta-yards

Crawl Space — *opens to a 16" mesh and plastic square, but folds to a 2' x 2' package with handle. Use indoors or out up to age twenty months.*

> Crawl Space
> P.O. Box 12009
> Cincinnati OH 45212 USA
> 1-800-543-8800 (Operator 710)

Kiddie Yard — *wood frame with vertical slats. Folds for travel or storage. (Approximately 12' square.) Use indoors or out up to twenty-four months. This company also makes doorway gates — several kinds — fixed or pressure type.*

> Nu-Line Industries
> Suring WI 54174 USA

Index

LA LECHE LEAGUE MEMBERSHIP

As you read through the pages of this book, you'll notice several references to La Leche League. La Leche League was founded in 1956 by seven women who had learned about successful breastfeeding while nursing their own babies. They wanted to share this information with other mothers. Now over 9,000 League Leaders and 3,500 League Groups carry on that legacy. League Leaders are always willing to answer questions about breastfeeding and mothering and are available by phone for help with breastfeeding problems. League Groups meet monthly in communities all over the world to share breastfeeding information and mothering experiences.

When you join LLL, you participate in an international mother-to-mother helping network, a valuable resource for parenting help and support. Your annual membership fee of $20.00 brings you six bimonthly issues of NEW BEGINNINGS, a magazine filled with stories, hints, and inspiration from other breastfeeding families. Members receive our LLLI Catalogues by mail and they are entitled to a 10% discount on purchases from LLLI's wide variety of outstanding books and publications on breastfeeding, childbirth, nutrition, and parenting.

Why should you join La Leche League? Because you care—about your own family and about mothers and babies all over the world!

Return this form to La Leche League International.
P.O. Box 1209, Franklin Park, IL 60131-8209 USA.

_____ I'd like to join La Leche League International. Enclosed is my annual membership fee of $20.

_____ In addition, I am enclosing a tax-deductible donation of $_____ to support the work of La Leche League.

_____ Please send me a copy of THE WOMANLY ART OF BREAST-FEEDING, softcover, $7.95 plus $1.50 for shipping and handling. *(In California and Illinois, please add sales tax.)*

_____ Please send me La Leche League's FREE Catalogue.

_____ Please send me a FREE copy of the Directory of LLL representatives. *(Please enclose a self-addressed, stamped envelope.)*

_____
Name

_____
Address

_____
State/Province   Zip/Postal Code   Country

7/85